BROKEN SILENCE

Memories of two Dutch Sisters,

Their Jewish Heritage, the War

and Rebuilding of Their Lives

GW00391564

Betty Bausch-Polak

Liesje Auerbach-Polak

Translated from:
Hebrew: *HaSheket SheNishbar.*
German: *Bewegtes Schweigen*
Dutch: *Bewogen Stilte*

ISBN 978-965-7542-18-7

Order Information:
This book is available through: www.Lulu.com or by writing to
E-mail: tsurtsinapublications@gmail.com

Tags: Dutch Jewry; Amsterdam; 2nd World War; WWII, persecution; Westerbork; Bergen-Belsen; hiding; Holocaust; Holocaust survivor; German Templers; Aliyah Beth; Atlit; War of Independence; Righteous Gentiles; Hadassah Hospital; Eilat; Germany; resistance; Extermination Camp, Transit Camp, Israel, British Mandate Palestine; Hebrew; Mount Scopus;

Photos: Betty Bausch and Liesje (Elisheva) Auerbach
and internet (free domain).

A *Tsur Tsina* Production
Lay-out: Petra van der Zande

Printed by Printiv, Jerusalem, Israel

Dedicated to our parents,

Whose ashes were scattered.

With eternal gratitude

for the life they gave us.

Our parents, Griet and Frederik, just before their wedding, ca. 1909

Together with our parents in the Bussum forest. Liesje (l.) and Betty (r.) ca. 1928

CONTENTS

Introduction Liesje	6
Introduction Betty	8
Prewar 1933-1940	10
Occupied Netherlands	28
Bergen-Belsen	79
Hiding Together	100
British Mandate Palestine	115
Netherlands—Partially Liberated	118
Philip	129
The Search for Survivors	134
British Mandate Palestine	139
Jewish State - *Eretz Israel*	158
Hans Auerbach	161
Second Marriage Betty	168
A Different Germany	172
Epilogue	175
Acknowledgements	178
Index	179

INTRODUCTION LIESJE*

*"Liesje" is pronounced as 'lees-yah'

Our warm and loving parental home was situated in the Plantage neighborhood in the center of Amsterdam where my sister and I shared eighteen years of joy and sorrow. We had a close bond during those wonderful years of our youth. Then the war came. We both survived.

Betty remained in the Netherlands, and I ended up in British Mandate Palestine. While each lived a completely different life we kept in touch by a lively correspondence - much of which has been preserved. I married, and had children and grandchildren.

One seldom sees two sisters who are so very different, yet who do things in precisely the same way and experience things so similarly. For example, neither of us finds it easy to throw things away. This explains the fact that we have both saved much of our correspondence over more than seventy years. After a long separation our lives are finally united once again, in Israel.

The war affected our lives, and although I should like nothing better than to put it all behind me once and for all, it has proved impossible to forget.

My husband and I did our best to raise our two sons as free, self-confident Israelis. Above all we had no wish to turn them into "Second Generation" children, burdened with the tragic remembrances of their parents.

Then came the Eichmann trial in 1961 in Jerusalem. Our sons followed it closely, and it dawned upon them what had happened to the Jews of Europe and its implications.

They knew now what we had been through and that we were counted among the few who had been spared the terrible fate suffered by millions of others. Until that point we had kept silent, and our sons had not asked. It was as though we had made an unspoken agreement not to talk about the Holocaust.

However, with the third generation the great silence was broken. The grandchildren would not leave us alone. They began to ask questions, which we gradually answered.

We thank our sons for understanding our silence, and we thank the grandchildren for being the right ones to unlock our hearts. Steven Spielberg succeeded in getting my husband to talk. Proceeds of his movie, "Schindler's List" were used to seek out and interview Holocaust survivors all over the world. Many were persuaded to record their life history on camera so their suffering would never be forgotten.

Thanks are also due to all those who encouraged me to write this book, my husband first and foremost.

My sister Betty kept all my letters over the decades. Especially the correspondences from 1944-1946, when I worked in Hadassah Hospital in Jerusalem, became the foundation stones of this book.

INTRODUCTION BETTY

At an advanced age, my sister Liesje and I began writing down our memories of the Second World War, which had been suppressed until well into the 1980's. We both sought to begin afresh with a new life, unencumbered by the burdens of the past. People who had not experienced it could not possibly comprehend the enormity of it all.

When I agreed to be interviewed on the "Dutch Evangelistic Broadcasting" (Evangelische Omroep) by Pim van der Hoff in the Netherlands, the unexpected reactions from acquaintances and total strangers and the emotions that rose to the surface made it clear that the time had come to tell the next generation about the past. Yet still, it took over ten years before I could bring myself to put my life story down on paper.

What encouraged me was the biography of my childhood friend, Benno Gitter, published in both Hebrew and English. The publication in the year 2000 of "Steal a Pencil for Me", where my brother Jaap (Jack) and Ina relate the fascinating tale of their love as it blossomed in the Westerbork and Bergen-Belsen camps had a great impact on us.

Pim van der Hoff's suggestion that my sister and I each write down our memories of the war and combine them in one book was an enormous stimulus. But it was Liesje, more than anyone else, who continually pushed me.

We Polak sisters each have a completely different story to tell. Liesje, the younger sister, was released from the Bergen-Belsen concentration camp in a prisoner exchange between Jewish inmates of the camp and the German Templars who had been living in Palestine. She arrived in British Mandate Palestine in July of 1944. Her story is one of single-minded determination, optimism and luck. One may even call it a miracle.

Philip de Leeuw and I married in December 1939. He enlisted in the army, and after the Germans conquered the Netherlands in May 1940, we attempted three times to flee to England, but failed. A few years later, when it became impossible to live as Jews, we changed our identities and found hiding places. Philip joined the Resistance, was captured and executed in November 1944. I survived the war. All that I have been through has made me into what I am today.

Despite the calamities that befell us, after the war the three surviving Polak siblings made a comeback to life in every sense of the word. Liesje, who had to start a new life all alone, built a family and a successful career in Israel. My brother Jaap (Jack), who was a mere skeleton upon liberation from the concentration camp, went on to raise a wonderful family in the U.S.A I established a fascinating and fulfilling life in Holland and other countries. Every foundation had been completely destroyed, but we raised ourselves up from the rubble. This is our story.

PRE WAR 1933-1940

Betty

When I was 19 years old I left Amsterdam, the city of my birth, never to live there again. I returned now and then only for visits. The once-so-picturesque Jewish neighborhoods were crisscrossed by broad highways and flanked by pompous, high-rise buildings. Walking there, I feel haunted by the shadows of dear ones, forcibly removed from their homes and deported, never to return.

In the embrace of a warm and happy family I enjoyed a sheltered childhood. My wonderful, dearly beloved parents, Frederik and Griet were always there for us. Juul was my eldest sister, Liesje the younger one, and Jaap (Jack) my 6-year older brother.

In the Netherlands, the financial crisis already began to be felt in 1927. When Hitler came to power in Germany in 1933, my teenage years became increasingly overshadowed by the rise of National Socialism. From the very first days we were confronted with the bitter ramifications of the policies of this new government: the ever-rising stream of Jewish refugees from Germany. My parents, who were always mindful of the sufferings of others, offered help where they could. Many times I stood in the doorway of an impoverished home, holding bowls of food. These people were highly civilized and cultured. The ground had been swept out from under their feet, shattering their lives. I felt their humiliation keenly and always fled as fast as I could, embarrassed and troubled by their gratitude.

Our parents in the garden of their last home in Amsterdam, Plantage Franschelaan.
After the war this street was renamed: Henri Polaklaan

If these cultured and educated people, scientists, artists, the pillars of society had to flee, leaving everything behind to save their lives, I concluded that Hitler was the greatest possible danger to society. When his ranting, raving speeches blasted everywhere through the radio, my heart shivered with fear and foreboding. Unfortunately, I was among the few who took him seriously when he shouted "Jews are the rats of the world, they all have to be destroyed". The threats and torrents of abuse were so perverse that people refused to listen to him. There were those who sought to calm me down, saying: "Oh, stop taking everything so seriously", and buried their own heads in the sand. But from the first time I heard that man hollering his nauseating abuse, I had no doubt that he would carry out his threats. The signs were so patently obvious. Even my altruistic, good-hearted parents knew this but they believed firmly that it was wrong to abandon others in order to save your own life. This belief led them to their deaths.

The impending catastrophe crept nearer and nearer. I was 18 years old when the cinema newsreel showed Neville Chamberlain, the Prime Minister of England, shaking hands with Hitler –I shuddered. This pact, we were made to believe, would bring peace to Europe. In fact it came at the expense of Czechoslovakia. By means of a treacherous pact this quiet, peaceful country was 'sold' to Germany. The realization that all of Europe was in danger shot through me like a bolt of lightning. It was a turning point in my life. In the silent cinema I and a few others, mostly youngsters, jumped up and began to boo and hiss, cursing Chamberlain, Hitler, the Nazis - and all those who cooperated with them. From that moment I realized that I could not run with the crowd, I had to sound the alarm and persuade others to take action.

Left to right: Betty, Liesje, Jaap (Jack), Juul

The Polak children

We were a very warm, close-knit family, Orthodox Jewish, though not rigidly so, living happily in the Plantage neighborhood in Amsterdam.

Religion in our home was consistent in that we always festively observed all the regulations and traditions of Judaism.

The most special moment in the week was on Friday evening when Father blessed each one of us. I can still feel his tender hands on my hair, and remember the intensity of his murmured prayer that ended with a loud: "May God bless you and protect you, Amen."

How significant these words have become to me in light of the time gone by.

The entire family sat together around the table for a traditional Sabbath meal. We sang Sabbath hymns, among them those of the poet Chaim Nachman Bialik, who was a favorite of my father's.

The Jewish festivals were the high point of the year. For Sukkoth, the autumn Feast of Tabernacles, we built a sukkah (a booth) out of wood and reeds on the terrace of the fourth floor bathroom. The elongated room had an enormous wooden table, surrounded by benches. It provided enough sitting place for three families at once. We ate all our meals there throughout the holiday, amidst a constant coming and going of guests.

In the weeks before Passover, the house was thoroughly scrubbed and polished. Not a single crumb of bread could be found. To commemorate the Exodus of Israel from Egypt we ate matzos instead of the usual yeast bread. At the special Seder meal on Passover eve the story was narrated in the traditional manner. At least 20 people would be seated around the festive table with the blue porcelain service that was taken out only one time in the year.

Such memories…

Priestly blessing ~ Numbers 6: 24-26

May the LORD (YHWH) bless you and guard you -

יְבָרֶכְךָ יהוה, וְיִשְׁמְרֶךָ

("Yebhārēkh-khā Adhōnāy weyishmerēkhā …")

May the LORD make His face shed light upon you and be gracious unto you -

יָאֵר יהוה פָּנָיו אֵלֶיךָ, וִיחֻנֶּךָּ

("Yā'ēr Adhōnāy pānāw ēlekhā wiḥunnékkā …")

May the LORD lift up His face unto you and give you peace -

יִשָּׂא יהוה פָּנָיו אֵלֶיךָ, וְיָשֵׂם לְךָ שָׁלוֹם

("Yissā Adhōnāy pānāw ēlekhā wiyāsēm lekhā shālōm.")

Liesje

Looking back over my life I have memories of a wonderful youth in Amsterdam, a vibrant city, full of action. We lived on the top three floors of a typical row house in the Plantage Kerklaan, diagonally opposite the Artis Zoo: father, mother and four children. I was the youngest. My parents' first child, Meir, had died of kidney disease at the age of two. They didn't talk about him but I have one photo where he looks sweet and beautiful. Jaap (Jack), born after him, was very spoiled. With three younger sisters in the family he felt no need to help with housework. "The girls can do that," he would say.

Juul, the eldest of the girls, was quiet and no trouble to her parents. She became a teacher at a Jewish school in Amsterdam. I regret that the eight years between us prevented me from getting to know her better.

My connection with Betty, who was three years older than I, was always closer. We were the 'little ones' in the family. Betty was full of life and energy, a strong personality who chose her own path in life without allowing other's opinions to take preference over her own. Perhaps her stubbornness and persistence is what saved her life. I was the opposite, easy-going and cheerful, trying to get along with others.

These were the Polak children.

Father was a special man, always concerned for those who suffered in times of crisis. He was a clever accountant, but through some 'flaw of character' he sometimes forgot to send out bills for his work. "These people have a hard enough life as it is," he said.

Mother was an energetic, hardworking, intelligent woman, and a well-known teacher. She met Father when he signed up for her shorthand class, but also taught handiwork at my primary school. One year, Mother taught the class I was in, and when a few girls didn't like handicraft, I finished their projects to give my mother the impression our class was the best of the school.

My religious education influenced my life deeply. When I was about six years old and had done something that was forbidden, Father asked if I was responsible.

"No," I said, "I didn't do that."

"Please, come along with me," Father calmly said.

We walked to the street corner where there were no trees, and he said: "Look up, to God, and then tell me again whether you did it or not. "It's hard enough to lie to your father, but to God? No, I couldn't. I hung my head and confessed,

"Father, I did it to help Mother."

Betty and Grandmother in Artis, 1930

Every Friday morning Grandmother, who lived right on the corner of the Muidergracht, came to prepare the Sabbath meal. She was a short woman who wore her grey hair in a bun, and was always dressed in many layers of black clothes. The way she swung her mahogany walking stick made her look like royalty. Her high boots were black and she always carried a black bag in which she kept a small box of mints. Each child received one and only after we had washed our hands. Sitting at the big kitchen table I watched the recurrent ritual: the meatballs for the soup were rolled first; then the apple cake and the *kugel* were baked. During this time the delicious smell of chicken soup, slowly cooking on a small paraffin stove, filled the kitchen. Already at a young age we learned the rules about *kashrut* – kosher food. We would never eat meat and milk together, and pork was strictly forbidden.

The nearby Artis Zoo enriched our childhood. All the Polak children could be found there at any free moment. Thanks to our membership, we could visit the zoo even on Sabbath when we were not allowed to handle money. The famous Dr. Anton Portielje took us on exciting excursions, sometimes even in the dark - after visiting hours. On the weekends Father joined us and on the spot composed funny rhymes about the animals. It was great fun.

My parents were very open-minded for their day and age, but not enough to speak to us about sex. I even had no idea what the word meant. When a doctor who was a close friend of my parents died, they took care of his belongings. Among the books they brought home was one on sexual education, which soon disappeared. I later discovered it hidden under Juul 's mattress. When she was not at home I surreptitiously read the book and thus received my sexual education.

The years went by. Jaap (Jack) married a sweet girl who had come to the Netherlands from Russia with her mother. But Jaap (Jack) and Manja were not at all compatible. Years later, when I asked Manja why she had agreed to the marriage, she answered simply, "I loved your father so much, that I could not bring myself to disappoint him." My eldest sister, Juul , married shortly after, and so did Betty.

During a Mizrachi Summer Camp in Oosterbeek, about 1937 . From left to right: Benno Gitter, Betty, Liesje, Bram Pais and Jaap (Jack)

Betty

It was taken for granted that we would join the Mizrahi Youth Organization, the religious branch of the Zionist Movement that sought to establish an independent state in Palestine, where Jews would live free from the fear of persecution. It was a time of great concern. The sword of Damocles was already hanging over our heads.

Father had become a member of the Mizrahi organization as soon as it was founded. In an old photograph from the 1920's, he is pictured together with the great Zionist, Chaim Weizmann, during his visit to Holland.

Father with Chaim Weizmann, who was to become the first President of Israel.

Weizman   Father

The goal of the Zionist movement was to restore the Jewish people to their historic land, Palestine. Towards the end of the 19[th]century the nationalistic goal became political: to establish a legally assured and independent homeland. It was Theodor Herzl who propagated this idea in 1897 at the First Zionist Congress in Basel. Following this, the Jewish National Fund was established in 1901, and proceeded to purchase land from the Arabs. The expanding Jewish possession of the land was legitimized by the Balfour Declaration of 1917, in

Betty and Liesje on their way to
Summer Camp 1937

which the British rulers of Palestine promised the Jews an independent state. "The Promised Land" was no cliché, it was a real promise.

As ardent idealists, we took part in all the activities, and never missed one of the summer camps in the village of Garderen in central Holland. Modern Hebrew as well as the *Tanach* (the Hebrew Bible), the history of the Jewish people and the Holy Land were studied intensively. In short, the youth movement filled our lives. The logical step further was to prepare ourselves to be pioneers in Palestine, which was then under the British Mandate. Once thoroughly trained, we would be able to help build up the land.

It was a fascinating time. I acquired a great deal of knowledge from the lively discussions in our meetings and I have no doubt that my cultural development was, to a large extent, formed there. A great many of those in the movement, my compatriots who survived the war, rose to important positions in society and in the State of Israel.

It was in the youth organization that I met Philip, my future husband, an economics student at the Amsterdam University. Although he was deeply interested in economics and politics, it was chiefly his love of nature that attracted me to him.

At the time I was studying to become a teacher of Jewish religion, out of respect and love to my father, though in reality my orthodox upbringing was beginning to unravel.

Philip (Flip) as a student, ca. 1939

Preparing to become a pioneer in Palestine, I had to learn all kind of skills, called *Hachshara*, which for me meant working as a house maid in a family blessed with several children.

I felt out of place and unhappy there and was therefore over-joyed to be accepted at both a market garden and a small dairy farm where I milked the cows early in the morning. At long last I could work outdoors.

My fiancé, Philip, gave up his studies for a master's degree and also began to work on a farm. In our innocence and na-ïveté we were convinced that intellectuals would be of little use in a country that needed to be built up from the ground. First and foremost, so we were told, skilled labor would be needed, people who could roll up their sleeves and work.

A group of our friends, who had finished their training, had left for Palestine to establish a *kibbutz* in the north. Kibbutz Chuliot was later renamed Sde Nehemia. Most of the members of this kibbutz were from the Netherlands.

My life was full of contrasts. Once a week I traveled some 30 kilometers from the farm where I worked in Eemnes to the Royal Concert hall in Amsterdam. In the ladies' powder room

 I would change out of my work trousers into a winered, velvet evening dress. However, at six o'clock on the dot the next morning I was back at my milking stool. Leaning my head against the cow's warm body, last night's music played over and over in my mind.

Liesje

Like Betty, I wished to be trained to help build a homeland for the Jewish people. For the most part this *hachshara* included agriculture, gardening and the construction professions.

I graduated from High School in 1940, the year Holland fell under Nazi occupation. Every day new German decrees were issued, blocking the paths of Jewish students who wished to pursue higher studies. On my father's advice I began work in an accounting firm. But I soon decided to go on to *hachshara*. That is how I arrived at the large market garden of the van der Weide family in Sloterpolder, a village on the outskirts of Amsterdam.

Liesje (ri) at the market garden of the van der Weide family, 1941

Every day I rode my bicycle eight kilometers from the Plantage to the farm and back. When the decrees against the Jews became increasingly stringent and we were forced to turn in our bicycles, I had to walk the entire distance. Then the Germans ordered all Jews to wear a yellow star, inscribed with the word 'JOOD' (Jew) sewn visibly on our clothes. I walked to and from the farm, an hour and a half in each direction, with the yellow star prominently displayed on my coat lapel.

There were several farms in the area. Everyone knew everyone else, and no difference was felt between Jews and non-Jews. It was a wonderful time, mainly thanks to the van der Weide family who received me with unusual warmth and kindness, and their three sons who worked with us in the vegetable garden after school. When their daughter, Julia, was born I was invited to the festive christening ceremony. This was the first time in my life I had ever set foot inside a church. In light of everything that happened later, I may have idealized my time in the Sloter Polder. I was working there with a goal in mind: to train myself for immigration to Palestine and to evade the clutches of the occupiers.

Many years later, when visiting the Sloterpolder again, the village no longer existed. It had been swallowed up by the big city. The quaint village houses had been replaced by blocks of flats and impersonal buildings.

A few years ago I was interviewed by a Dutch magazine. My story sounded familiar to a reader. She asked her husband if he knew the woman in the photo. "No", he said, looking at the picture of a woman in her fifties. But when he saw the second picture of his father in Sloterpolder he cried out, "That is our Liesje!" They made enquiries and found me in Israel. We have been in touch ever since.

Betty

As a reserve officer in the Infantry Reserves, my fiancé, Philip, had been called into active service in April of 1939. He became commander of the Border Control Unit in Dinxperlo and the surrounding area. Dinxperlo is a village on the border with Germany; a dull, sleepy town whose only distinction is that the main shopping street forms the border between Germany and the Netherlands. The Dutch in Dinxperlo lived on the west side and the Germans on the east side of the street. The inhabitants spoke a mixture of both languages which no one else understood.

Since Philip and I missed each other terribly, we decided to get married that same year on December 21, 1939. The Great New Synagogue of Amsterdam, where the traditional wedding took place, was packed to capacity. Philip wore his military uniform and I was a demure bride behind a veil.

Lots of young people were present, most of them friends from the Zionist youth movement. When the impressive ceremony was concluded the young people enthusiastically sang

HaTikvah, "The Hope", at the top of their voices, much to the consternation of the adults who had nothing to do with any Zionistic aspirations. This was the first time the hymn had been sung in the synagogue! The local head rabbi got up and stalked out of the room in anger. Many adults reacted with cries of "For shame!" Protest letters continued to pour into the office of the local Jewish Weekly for many weeks afterwards.

Because of the state of security Philip was not permitted to leave the country. We had to spend a miserable three-day honeymoon in The Hague in the freezing cold of December - not something we would have chosen to do had we been given a choice. Back at his border post Philip was kept busy with his officer duties. And I was bored to death in our two rented rooms in the small, sleepy village of Breedenbroek, near Dinxperlo.

In an effort to combat the boredom we took fencing lessons and hiked in the beautiful woods around us. Nevertheless, time went by slowly. Philip, who loved nature and hiking, volunteered for long marches with his soldiers, for which he earned extra leave. Being an energetic, lively twenty-year-old, it wasn't easy to be far away from my family and friends and cut off from the vibrant life of the big city. I decided to learn horseback riding, as my soldier husband had been taught in the army. But Philip declared, "We don't have the money to pay for that!"

Having always been independent and opinionated, I was forced to draw a line here; otherwise there would have been trouble in the future. The way I resolved this issue would affect the rest of my married life.

"I'm going to Amsterdam to earn money for the riding gear and lessons," I informed my husband.

My wonderful parents accepted me without a word of protest. A month later, I returned to Philip and began my riding lessons.

This decision had two favorable outcomes: first of all, our rides together with his friends in the beautiful area around Breedenbroek became an enjoyable pastime for Philip and me. Secondly, from then on all the decisions in our marriage were made together.

In effect, I have my parents to thank for my insistence on this matter. They were considered very open-minded for their day. My mother's father (whom sadly I never met), had raised his children – both girls and boys – in full equality. All seven were educated so that they could earn their own living. He allowed them to learn all kind of sports like swimming, gymnastics and rowing and they each had a bicycle.

My mother was a working woman - a teacher, and independent – something quite rare in those days. We never complained if we didn't find her at home when we returned from school. On the contrary, we raided the cookie jar and ran outside to play in the nearby zoo.

By the end of April 1940, tensions increased and Philip and his men were stationed at the Grebbeberg in the centre of the Netherlands, where the Dutch had built the main line of defense.

OCCUPIED NETHERLANDS

Betty

It was a beautiful, sunny spring day on May 10, 1940 when war broke out in the Netherlands. The entire country was blooming with new life. But nature did not reflect the reality.

The heavy fighting on the Grebbeberg resulted in innumerable casualties. After a week of fierce battles, the Netherlands surrendered.

In Dinxperlo, far from the action, not a single German soldier appeared and we were deprived of any news. There was no transportation, no radio, telephone lines were not working and no post was delivered. We could only guess what was happening in the rest of the country.

Anxious and unhappy I helped the farmers milk their cows, keeping as busy as I could. Ten days later, on another sunny morning, I saw a crowd of villagers approaching. The postman in front, waving a piece of paper, shouted, "A telegram from Philip, he is alive and well!"

The whole village knew the glad tidings before I did.

Philip was demobilized on June 15th. As a Jew, there was no question of whether or not he should surrender as a Prisoner of War and entrust himself to the protection of the Geneva Convention. For him there were only two possible courses of action: either to flee to England and join the Allied Forces or to go into hiding and try to fight the Germans from inside.

"There. You see, it's not so bad, is it?" people said at the beginning of the occupation. It was true, the Germans behaved with correctness. At first the decrees against the Jews were hardly felt. We all wanted to believe in the basic decency of the conquerors and to relax our guard.

But quietly, inexorably, one by one decrees were enacted to hand in our radios, bicycles and jewelry. Property was confiscated; we were banned from our beloved pursuits, from work places and from occupations that were vital to our existence and self-esteem. The "Jews Forbidden" edicts – which denied us entry to shops, sports facilities, swimming pools and parks, and the curfew that forced us to stay indoors after 8:00 p.m. –these were all direct assaults on my freedom-loving spirit.

When the order came to register as Jews I was determined not to submit to it. This registration could only be in the interest of the occupier. In this way the enemy would learn who we were and where we lived. Philip and many others thought differently, believing that as Jews we had to remain true to our identity and could not deny our faith. Before I was aware of it, he had registered us both.

But I sensed the deception behind the "Declaration of Aryan Identity", which civil servants were obliged to sign. Clearly only non-Jews could sign this paper. Anyone who did not was, in effect, declaring his Jewish identity. From the moment I understood that, I was possessed by one thought alone: how to stay out of the clutches of the Germans!

Acting differently from the mainstream, I didn't turn in my bicycle, hid the radio we had been ordered to hand over, and avoided wearing the yellow star as much as possible. Whenever I could get away with it, I refused to follow orders.

From April 1942, Dutch Jews were forced to wear the Yellow star with "JOOD" (Jew). Signs appeared with "Forbidden for Jews".

The center for *hachshara* was in Deventer. Ru Cohen and his wife, Eef, were the enthusiastic leaders of the training. We decided to settle there for the

Betty in the cucumber hothouse in Twello 1941

time being, and were lucky to find an apartment to rent from a dance teacher in a quaint old house on the Oude Market in the very center of Deventer. Philip found work at the *hachshara* center in Ru Cohen's office. I was given work in the market garden 'De Ziele' in Twello about seven kilometers from Deventer, to which I rode my bicycle every day. Although I was just a field- hand, the youngest and the only female in a male world, I felt very fortunate. The owner, Jansen, gave us valuable information, taking the time to explain as much as he could. He taught us a great deal about horticulture and encouraged us to expand our knowledge by private study. At the time I had no idea how useful this knowledge would be to me in my future vocation.

One day I was riding my bike on the narrow bridge over the IJssel River when I was shoved aside by a horse and buggy and hurt my ankle. I kept on working, for in our *hachshara* we were taught to steel ourselves to work hard, to ignore pain and keep going. Ten days later I was in the hospital. It was a hard lesson for me, as I now had to suffer the inconvenience of a plaster cast for six weeks. Luckily for me, I could pass this time in the home of Ru Cohen's brother. There I forged a close friendship with Trude Cohen[1] and her mother, Hede, who lovingly cared for me.

[1] Trude, her husband Jacques and son Ernst, who was later engaged to my sister Liesje, did not survive the war. Only the youngest child, Ruth, and grandmother, Hede, were spared.

Liesje

This year we observed *Yom Kippur*, the holiest day of the Jewish calendar, as we did every year - with fasting and prayer. The Day of Atonement, prayers consecrated to God, a day to ask and receive forgiveness. The day of prayer begins after sunset on the eve of this High Holy Day. We went to the synagogue of the Zichron Ya'acov youth movement, whose members were mainly young people with hopes for the future, people with their faces turned towards Palestine, strong people who would build her up. The Sabbath and High Holy Day services in the synagogue were led by the young men and had a unique atmosphere. The cantors who stood before the ark were blessed with wonderful voices.

A shadow of dejection and anxiety lay over us all on this *Yom Kippur*. In contrast to former years, people were sunk deep in thought and in prayer. We were concerned for everyone, not just for ourselves. In July the hunt had begun. So many had already been taken away. Deep in our hearts we felt that this would be our last Day of Atonement together.

The cantor or "*chazzan*" for the early morning prayer, *Shacharit*, was David, a handsome young man with a pleasant voice. I loved listening to him, his chanting, and special poetry of this holy day. After reading from the Torah, Emil continued with the *Moussaf* prayer. Every word was intoned with devotion as if carved out of his heart. We were speaking directly to God. We asked, we pleaded, we cried out to Him, "Our Father, Our King, have mercy on us for we have no works. Show us righteousness and mercy and deliver us!"

The ancient words had deeper, more painful significance on this *Yom Kippur,* the last in the country of our birth. Emil, the wonderful *chazzan,* was able to rouse us. We felt as if the *shekhina*, the spirit of God, was with us in the synagogue. Surely, we told ourselves, the Holy One will hear these prayers from the depths of our hearts. The contrast between the sense of spiritual elevation in the inside and the cold reality on the outside caused incredible tension.

The afternoon prayer ended. Usually, there was a short break between the afternoon and evening prayers. But on that particular *Yom Kippur* we changed the tradition. We were afraid that the Germans would come to our houses that night to take us, and therefore decided to continue immediately with *Mincha*, the evening prayer, without stopping for a break. We had to finish the prayers early so that we would have time to eat something at home before we were taken away on a long journey to an unknown destination.

Towards the completion of the *Moussaf* prayer a messenger came into the synagogue bearing a message for Max, the eldest cantor in the synagogue. He was married and the father of two small children. After whispering a few words the messenger left. Max slowly rose and stood next to Emil. When the latter intoned the final words of the *Moussaf* prayer, he continued immediately with the *Mincha*. We understood then that our modest request for a postponement of deportation for just this one day had not been honored.

The cantor's prayer remains engraved on my memory. "*Yitgadal veYishtabach Shemay Raba*". He dwelled on every letter and emphasized each word as if he wanted to say: "Our Father our King, do you hear us? Hear our voice. Forgive us, Father, forgive our sins."

The *Mincha* prayer was immediately followed by the *Neila*, the closing prayer of the day. The Holy Ark that housed the scrolls of the Torah was opened, and we stood up before it, several hundred young people, murmuring the words of the prayer in trembling and devotion. We were wonderful youth - the generation of the future. But many were already missing from among us. Where had they been taken? What had become of them? Our thoughts for them, for ourselves, the bleak reality that had overtaken us, the solemn atmosphere of *Yom Kippur* and the words of the prayer – all these enveloped us with both despair and hope at the same time.

Tears streamed from our eyes as we wept unashamedly. "Open for us the gate at the time the gate is shut" we cried out. We were so young, and yet so old. "Hear O Israel, the Lord our God the Lord is One". Tears ran like rivers over our cheeks. "God!" I said within my heart, "I so much want to live, we all want to live. Help me, help us!"

There will never be another prayer like ours on that *Yom Kippur*. The blowing of the *shofar* ended the prayer of *Neila*, and was followed by a heavy, ominous silence. We wished each other 'gmar hatima tova', may you be inscribed in the Book of Life, and hurried home to the unknown.

Jewish Amsterdam, 1942

Did God hear my prayer? I was saved. I am alive. Why me? How was my prayer any different from that of David, or Emil, or Max and all the many others who never returned? Only God knows.

Betty

While working in De Ziele I registered for studies at the specialized school of fruit growing in Terwolde, not far from Deventer. There I was accepted under exceptional circumstances: firstly, as their first female student; secondly, without the necessary qualifications for acceptance – five years of experience in agriculture and a diploma from an agricultural school – and, finally, because I was Jewish.

During my studies the principal, Mr. Honig, ignored the order of the Nazi government to expel the Jewish student from his school for as long as he could. But a few weeks before the final exams, after a third warning and threat, he had no choice but to act, and quickly. Entering the class, he begged me to take my books and other belongings, for he had to dismiss me.

Outside, in parting, he said, "The day will soon come when I will personally hand you your Diploma". He handed me a small piece of paper. "Be very careful with this. Here is our address. Whenever you need help, you can come to our home, day or night".

If only more people had been like him. The family indeed received me and helped me during the war and directly after.

Once the war broke out it was no longer possible to flee to Palestine, although our immigration certificates were prepared and waiting for us in England. Bowing to Arab pressure the British, then ruling in Palestine, established an immigration quota. In effect this meant that the gates of the Land of Israel were slammed shut in the hour of our greatest need.

Philip's younger brother, Dries, had prepared an escape route to England with the help of his father, who had good connections in France. I scribbled down the route on pieces of cigarette paper, and memorized all the names and addresses we would need in our possible flight. For years I kept them hidden in my shoe.[1]

To our endless frustration and grief we could not flee using the route Dries had planned for us. We also failed three times in attempts to flee directly to England by boat. In the end we began to make serious preparations to go into hiding. On this we were of one mind: we would not let anyone deport us anywhere!

Going into hiding had serious consequences. It meant, in effect, that we would have to sever all ties with family and friends, take on new identities and, the worst by far, live separated from each other with no way of knowing for how long this would last.

Philip, who "looked" Jewish, had to find a place where he could more or less live out of sight. I, myself, would be able to work without anyone suspecting that I was, in fact, Betty Polak, a Jewess.

In the meantime we moved from Deventer to nearby Apeldoorn. Here, in May 1942, we were obliged for the first time to wear the yellow star I had until now refused to sew on to my clothes. We rented a room in an apartment near the asylum away from the center of town. In the Jewish psychiatric hospital "Apeldoornsche Bosch" we found work as gardeners, and although our pay was next to nothing, we were able to take our meals there and, if necessary, receive medical treatment.

---

[1] After months of travel by foot, train and bicycle, Dries managed to eventually reach England. It was a long journey through Belgium, France, Spain and Portugal and fraught with dangers. Once in England, Dries volunteered for the Royal Air Force and received training at the air force flight school in Canada. There he became an expert on Spitfires. In June of 1944, he participated in the invasion of Europe and later fought in Israel's War of Independence, one of the first pilots in the fledgling state's new Air Force, together with Ezer Weizmann.

When an edict was issued forbidding Jews to live with non-Jews, we moved in with the Querido family on the grounds of the psychiatric hospital.

Dr. Arie Querido had been a renowned psychiatrist in Amsterdam. Because of his Jewish ancestry he was considered Jewish. Removed from his position in the city he began working in the Apeldoornsche Bosch. His Aryan wife was a child psychiatrist. She did not work in the Jewish hospital and was often away. So, in return for their kindness, I took it upon myself to help with the housework and the care of their two children, a boy and a girl.

It was a unique experience working with mentally ill people, in the gardens as well as the household. It required compassion and a great deal of patience.

We lived relatively peacefully in the large villa of this "mixed couple". Various performances and lectures were held in the large auditorium. The height of delight for me was listening to the piano playing of one of the patients, Misha Hillesum.

Many a time I would secretly slip away from my gardening work into the auditorium where a fragile figure, completely withdrawn into himself, sat alone on the enormous stage improvis-

Philip and Betty taking a break while working in the "Apeldoornsche Bosch", Summer 1942

ing, composing music as if from heaven. For hours, at any and every possible opportunity, I could have listened to him. The famous conductor Mengelberg, respected by the Nazis, tried to save Misha[1], who since his youth was called 'the second Mozart'. The Germans were willing to save his unique talent, but not his family members. By choosing to stay with his family, they all perished.

Philip and I lived peacefully in the Querido home, at this large institution surrounded by expansive vegetable gardens, flower beds and bee hives. Despite the constant tension and suspense I remember it as a pleasant time. But this was not to last long.

In the beginning of January 1943, the highest ranking SS commander in The Netherlands, Aus der Fünten, arrived from Amsterdam in order to personally oversee the deportation of all the inhabitants. Dr. Querido had to show him around and thus was made aware of what was going to happen. He did all he could to warn everyone possible of the terrible things that awaited them. How touching it was to hear the reactions of many of the staff, "We will remain with the patients; that is our responsibility."

January 13, 1943 was the last day we would be able to escape, and we hurriedly left under protection of darkness. Long cattle cars were already waiting in the Apeldoorn train station for the mass deportation to begin.

[1] Misha's older sister, Etty Hillesum, became famous when her diary was discovered. Her book *Het verstoorde leven* ("The Disturbed Life") was translated in many languages and adapted for theater plays. Like Misha did with his compositions, Etty too created a world of her own to hide from the horrors she experienced. Misha´s discovered compositions have rekindled interest. His Dutch biography was published and recordings of his piano music are now available.

After we left the institution on this cold winter night, all the inmates were dragged outside. No one was spared – the seriously ill, the mentally ill, handicapped, nurses, doctors, kitchen staff, visitors – all were hauled into lorries. It all went very quickly – people were shoved into the cattle cars by the terrible `Black` Dutch police. The train leaving Apeldoorn had one destination: the extermination camps.

The Queridos were allowed to return to their home in Amsterdam, not only because his wife was non-Jewish, but because he himself could prove descent from a partly Jewish, distinguished Sephardic family. We stayed in touch, during and after the war.

The Apeldoornsche Bosch
www.oud-apel

Liesje

Walking the streets with a conspicuous yellow star sewn onto my clothes was dangerous.

It marked me as different. We were not fully aware of the dreadful implications of the matter, though we did feel the danger. I knew all too well that my freedom would soon come to an end.

I was afraid. So were my parents. The increasing raids and Jew hunting in Amsterdam worried them. Something might happen on my daily walk to the training farm. In the end I decided not to take any more chances.

A short while later I began working as a student nurse in

the Netherlands Jewish Hospital close to our house. I had never for a moment considered a career in nursing but what choice did I have when the possibility of higher education was shut off to me? I couldn't imagine at the time that this quirk of fate would be the beginning of a long and successful career in nursing.

After a difficult day of work in the hospital I was relieved when my shift ended at four o'clock in the afternoon and I could go home. I was off duty until the next day's evening shift. The anticipation of a night in my own bed sped my steps on the short walk home.

I was weary. The night shifts were especially difficult and I desperately needed to recoup my strength at my parent's home before the next shift.

The weariness was not only from hard work, but above all from the constant pressure under which we lived. Not a moment went by when we could not sense our complete isolation, even in the midst of Amsterdam. The tension was sometimes unbearable.

After eight o'clock in the evening no one was allowed in the streets. That meant deserted streets, a tense stillness and the uncertainty of what that night would bring. When we woke in the morning our first thoughts were always,

"What do the Germans have planned for this evening?" and "Who will be their next victims?"

My mother and father enveloped me in love. I was their youngest daughter, the only one who had not been married. We sat together around the table, chatting about my brother and sisters, and I saw the deep concern for them in their eyes.

"Don't take it so hard", I managed to say, "It will all turn out all right."

Just moments later we heard sounds of a terrible commotion outside. There were shouts in German and the heavy stomping of boots. And then, the persistent ringing of the doorbell. Our turn had come. The moment we had feared so much. I said nothing but pointed upstairs with my finger as a sign that I would run upstairs. Mother understood immediately and nodded.

As fast as I could, I climbed up the stairs and crawled into a large, deep clothing cupboard. From outside you couldn't see how long and wide it actually was, and when you opened it you saw nothing but clothes. Cowering in the farthest corner I asked myself, "Is this the end? Will they find me? What is going to happen to me now?"

The inside of the closet was pitch-black, and I couldn't hear a thing going on outside.

I hardly dared breathe and had no idea how long I remained there, crouching in the corner.

In the meantime the Germans searched our house. They asked whether other people lived there and did not believe my parents when they said they lived alone. After a search downstairs, they walked up to the second floor. A soldier opened the door of the cupboard and shone a giant flashlight inside. Petrified, I prayed to God to save me. The beam of light shone towards me, went up and down over me and then continued. Just a few seconds, that's all it took, but for me it was an eternity. They did not discover me.

Sometime later, Mother came upstairs and opened the door.

"You can come out now", she said weakly.

"Where is Father?"

"They took him."

Betty

In the freezing January night from hell, Philip and I made our way through the dark forest. Our hearts, filled with grief and despair, told us what was happening in the asylum, Apeldoornsche Bosch.

We had prepared our flight carefully. Each of us took only one bag with basic essentials, for we had to walk long distances to avoid the main roads.

After a few hours we found the isolated farm where we could rest in a pig pen until the next morning. From there we walked to Amersfoort, and proceeded by train to Laren, a small city some 30 kilometers east of Amsterdam. We were familiar with Laren, where Philip's parents had lived in a villa before it was confiscated by the Dutch Nazis. There we could count on the help of good friends and thanks to our new identity papers we felt quite safe. According to my papers I was Jo Musch. From now on Philip was Philip van Andel. Luckily nobody along that route wanted to check our papers.

About 10 km from Laren a contact from the Resistance waited for us in Hilversum with two bicycles. The moment to part had come. Each of us had to ride alone to our new destination. From then on we had to give strangers the impression that we did not know each other. Jo Musch had never heard of Philip van Andel, and Philip van Andel had never heard of Jo Musch. Philip was brought to a more or less permanent address where he lived in hiding. He was not allowed to go outside anymore.

There was no difficulty in finding work for me, as I did not "look" Jewish thanks to my blue eyes. The place and its inhabitants where I worked to earn money had to be safe and preferably as close as possible to Philip. My first address in a big villa in Laren seemed to be all right.

During the next two and a half years before the liberation my identity changed often and I moved at least 20 times. Therefore I never had a chance to find out whether I was any good at my jobs as a farm hand, child nurse, housekeeper, cleaner, baby sitter, aide to the elderly, housemaid or social worker. I have always loved the theater and the little talent I had was brought to play in the various 'roles' I took on while in hiding and during confrontations with the authorities.

In the meantime I worked hard to improve my German. It became clear that when stopped at a checkpoint, something that happened quite frequently, the ability to speak the language of the occupier would be most useful, and could even save my life. Twice it happened that Jo Musch, using her best German at a checkpoint, was offered a job at the army command center. "Thank you, but I already have a job", she called out convincingly. The Betty in her grinned.

After a while I left my job in the big villa in Laren and became a milk maid at a farm. The cow shed on the farm was the only place where I could wash myself. Despite my best efforts to slip in there quietly, I was unable to escape the farmer's eye. When his attentions became too troublesome, the time came to move on. I found work on a farm in Twello, but there as well the farmer was too interested in his new milk maid. Perhaps he wasn't getting his way with his wife, who was pregnant with twins. The story I told him, that I was a married woman and my husband was a prisoner of war with the Germans, only excited him more. "You must be good at it! Show me!" he shouted at me. Surely he was not hinting at my milking abilities. After less than a week on that farm I had to look for other work.

The Germans gradually began to concentrate all of Holland's Jewry in Amsterdam. From there they were deported to the Westerbork concentration camp in the northeastern part of The Netherlands. It was a transit camp from which Jews were deported to the east. The city that provided refuge for the Spanish Jews in the 16th century was no longer safe for them in 1943. Nevertheless, when a position opened up at the Children's Home in the center of town, I didn't hesitate to return to Amsterdam.

It was dangerous to travel, particularly to Amsterdam. You always had to be on your guard and have a story ready on the tip of your tongue. In order to survive you had to develop a sixth sense about who you could trust and whom you should be aware of.

The trip from Deventer to Amsterdam went smoothly. It was quiet when I arrived at the central train station around 1 p.m. While descending the wide stairs towards the exit I noticed two men wearing raincoats – Secret Police (S.D.)! Having learned that attack was the best defence, I approached them.

"Oh, how wonderful to find somebody able to help me," I said in my best Deventer accent. "This is my first time in Amsterdam; I hear it's a very dangerous city. I'm here to visit my sick aunt." From my handbag I took an envelope with an address in the western part of the city - a non-Jewish area. "How can I get there safely?"

The two men explained which street car to take. Thanking them warmly I left the Central Station and hopped on the tram that would take me to my new hiding place, the Children's Home.

As it turned out, the Home was not the safest place for me, but it was the best one at that time. Only the director – mother of the well-known city photographer Colson – knew my true identity.

44

She supported her son, who had many useful contacts and helped a number of people in hiding. Besides her, no one else knew.

Regrettably, when I arrived at the Children's Home she was away for a few days. To my horror, my first duty was to accompany a group of children on the tram to a special school for the mentally handicapped in the Doklaan. It happened to be the street around the corner from where my parents lived, in the middle of the Plantage Quarter where I had been born and raised. Everybody knew me there!

"I won't do it!" I cried in my best Deventer accent, "I won't! The first time in my life in this dangerous city, alone with mentally handicapped children in the tram? Let's see what the Director has to say about that!"

The children in the Home came from different backgrounds. There were Jewish children living in hiding as well. The Director in her wisdom put me in charge of the Catholic children, who numbered about 20. This meant I had to pray with them at least three times a day and to accompany them to church on Sundays. How could I, a Jewish girl who had never seen the inside of a church, meet this challenge?

My solution was simple. I looked around a shop next door that sold religious articles. I told them of my relationship with a Catholic boy and how I was wondering what to do, as a Protestant, when I went to Mass with him next Sunday. By the time I emerged from the shop two hours later I had been fully prepared. The catechism echoed in my head, and in my hands I held a prayer book, a handbook about Catholic worship and a rosary.

The next Sunday a row of children walked in front of me towards the church. Betty Polak had become Jo Musch. On the other side of the street I suddenly noticed my cousin, Jaap

(Jack) Vecht, deep in thought, clearly wearing the yellow star. If he recognized me, I would be in grave danger. Quickly bending down to the child closest to me I exclaimed, "Oh, your shoelaces are loose! Halt everyone!" Crouching on the pavement I 'fixed' everyone's properly tied shoelaces until the danger had passed. In church, the children had to sit in the row before me for I didn't want anyone to see me making a mistake, even the smallest one.

Slowly I became familiar with the customs and prayers in Mass and my tensions somewhat eased. My work in the Home was very fulfilling. I was able to give the children the love and understanding they lacked, away from their parents and family. The love I missed, deprived of my husband, family and friends.

The Children's Home became too dangerous when Jo Musch became the unwitting target of a popular ditty sung. Before giving thanks for their dinner the children sang at the top of their voices, "Miss Jootje (Jo) is no Joodje (Jew), Miss Jootje is no Joodje." I had to leave. At the hour of departure a twelve year old boy who had grown very dear to my heart, gave me his silver rosary, his most precious possession.

In her false identity, Jo Musch found refuge with a very inter-esting family. The Althoffs lived in a spacious top-floor apart-ment on Stadhouderskade in central Amsterdam. When I ar-rived, a young Jewish couple, both well-known musicians, was hiding in the attic with their little boy. We were not the only ones who benefited from the hospitality of the Althoffs.

A long line of artists whose lives were in danger passed through this house. The Althoff family didn't ask for anything in return. As their baby's nurse and housemaid I was even given a monthly wage that was considered quite generous in those days: 30 Guilders! A short time before I had arrived in the Althoff home Eduard Althoff's only brother, Lex, had been arrested. Lex was a known journalist, one of the founders of the underground newspaper, *Het Parool* [1].

I avoided going outside for fear of bumping into acquaintances who knew that I was Jewish. But after the eight o-clock curfew, when Jews were forbidden to leave their houses, I dared to go out. After finding hiding places for my brother Jaap (Jack) and his wife Manja, I went to the southern part of Amsterdam where many Jews lived. Two white faces with large, terrified eyes stared back at me. Someone ringing the doorbell after eight o'clock could be none other than German soldiers taking them away.

Jaap (Jack) and Manja could not be persuaded that the only chance they had left was to go into hiding. "We don't want to be a burden to anyone", they insisted stubbornly. "We are young and strong and will have to work hard in the camps in Germany. But the war won't last much longer."

Discouraged and frustrated, I left their home.

Why was I unable to persuade anyone that the goal of the Nazis was to exterminate the entire Jewish race?

No. 51   5 APRIL 1943

HET PAROOL

VRIJ ONVERVEERD

DE ORGANISATIE VAN HET VERZET. | DAT IS RECHTSPRAAK!

[1] The Het Parool continues to be an important daily newspaper in Amsterdam, Netherlands.

Liesje

Hollandsche Schouwburg

Before their deportation to the East, the Jews who had been rounded up in Amsterdam were brought to a collection point in the Dutch Theater, the 'Hollandsche Schouwburg' (later called "The Jewish Theater"), and from there to Westerbork. My father was also taken to the Theater, but through the intervention of influential friends he was released and came home two days later, to our boundless joy.

But our luck was short-lived. Just one half year later my parents were arrested and deported directly to Westerbork. Every week I sent my parents all I could in order to make things easier for them, if only a bit. A never-ending fear for their safety continued to eat away at me. The information that filtered back to us about the camps in Eastern Europe filled us with horror. As the youngest of the four children, I was left desolate. I had lost my dear parents; the house was empty and my heart with it. But I was young and wanted to live. Working as a nurse gave meaning to my life.

August 13, 1943

It was a peaceful, sunny summer morning. As a second-year student nurse, I lived in the hospital's nurse's residence. That morning I had a lot of free time on my hands for the early shift didn't begin until ten o'clock. But the calm was rudely interrupted. At exactly eight o'clock a large convoy of lorries rumbled down our street in a show of power. One after the other the massive trucks pulled up in front of the Jewish hospital and within moments the compound was overrun by German soldiers who had come to evacuate all its inhabitants. Shouting and raging they entered the building. The auxiliary staff, the medical personnel and all of the patients were hauled off to the trucks. Watching in horror, I made a decision: I won't let them get me! I have to escape. But how? Hurrying from room to room, from ward to ward, I desperately searched for a place to hide until it was safe to leave the building while keeping up the appearance of being busy. Stunned patients were unceremoniously dragged from their beds; horrified doctors and nurses running helplessly, to and fro; and above the bedlam of shouts, cries, sobbing and pushing – the blood-curdling screeches of the German soldiers. While trying to find a hiding place they pushed patients toward me who had to be brought to the trucks. I kept running until I found myself on the attic. It was quiet there, and I began to hope that perhaps I would be able to get out of this horror alive. But I wasn't alone. The hospital architect, Mr. Baars and his three children were already hidden under the peak of the roof. My first thought was that the man who planned the building and knew every corner and crevice would certainly know the safest place to hide. I joined them. Mr. Baars happened to be at the hospital when he was on his way to drop the children off at school. The raid had taken him by surprise. We sat there as still as mice. The ten, eight and five-year-old children huddled close to each other in absolute silence. We listened to the roar of the engines and the lorries driving off with their screaming and wailing human cargo.

Seeing the small, frightened faces of the children, I descended the stairs, back to the commotion on the third floor. In the kitchen I grabbed a package of Zwieback and a few empty boxes for the children to relieve themselves.

It took ages before the noise of the last lorry faded away.

The hospital, usually full of hustle and bustle at all hours of the day or night, was eerily still. You could have heard a pin drop. It began to grow dark, but still we did not dare to creep out. Suddenly we heard footsteps and a harsh German voice call out, "We haven't been in here, yet!"

They climbed up to the attic. Hardly daring to breathe, we cringed, trying to make ourselves as small as possible. Wide, powerful beams of light played along the ceiling and over us.

"Please don't let them cough, please don't let them cry," I prayed, clutching the hand of two trembling children. Walking back and forth, the Germans came dangerously close to our hiding place. And then it was over.

As it was already past curfew, we decided to spend the night in the attic where we had the feeling to be completely alone in the large building. The next morning I sneaked downstairs to scout the area. A surrealistic atmosphere reigned in the hospital: vacant rooms and empty beds on the third floor. As I explored, it became evident that the Germans had left some nurses with foreign identity cards, and non-Jewish patients.

Guards were stationed at the entrance to the building. We couldn't get out without being discovered.

A nurse chanced upon me, she was startled when she recognized me. I told her about the attic. "If you want to escape," she whispered, "go over the roofs, but go quickly because the Germans are coming back in another hour!"

Mr. Baas and I decided to each go our own way.

Over the roof I climbed to the building next door. Luckily for me it was empty, but I understood sadly that its inhabitants had been deported. I ran down the stairs and slipped outside. What to do now? I asked myself, and decided to go to the home of my friend Ernst Cohen in the east end of Amsterdam. All I had was my nursing uniform.

Ernst's parents had been obliged to leave their big, beautiful home in Deventer where my sister Betty had lived for two months while her broken ankle was healing. Now they were living in a dilapidated flat in this ghetto of Amsterdam. Even though they received me with open arms, I felt superfluous. There was no privacy and I slept on the sofa in the living room. As I couldn't bring myself to live at someone else's expense, I began looking for work. The family was not religious and did not observe the Jewish traditions. For the first time in my life I had to eat non-kosher food. It was unbearable for me at first, but soon enough I got used to this new reality.

Ernst and I became a couple. We began to make preparations to go into hiding. In a few weeks we had expertly forged identity papers that would stand up to any scrutiny. We hid "emergency money", a twenty guilder banknote in a small crack in a cupboard, next to the forged papers. Having all we needed we now could look for a place to hide.

But it was too late.

It happened suddenly, without warning: the heavy tread of the boots, the shouts, the pounding on the door. Reading the list of names: Ernst, his parents, his sister and his grandmother.

"Be ready in half an hour", the soldier barked .

I was not on the list. Because I had escaped from the hospital I wasn't registered anywhere. As far as the Germans were concerned, I did not exist. Of course I could still escape with my valid identity card, but I couldn't abandon this family and Ernst.[1]

Out of my own free will, I went with them.

[1] Shortly after the liberation, Ernst died from typhus, malnutrition and total exhaustion on the "Lost Train" from Bergen-Belsen.

Betty

Despite my fear of leaving the house on Stadhouderskade, I ventured out several times to ride my bike to visit Philip, whom I missed terribly.

It was very difficult for him to adjust to life in his little room. He was never allowed to go outside, which made everything even harder as he was such a lover of the outdoors.

His friends supplied him with the books he needed to prepare for the Master's exams in Economics which he had decided to take after the war. As an agricultural economist he could contribute to Palestine. On large maps he followed the military movements meticulously. The knowledge that his parents and sister were also hidden in Laren was a great relief for him, even though he could not visit them. Each one was hiding at a different address.

Day by day Amsterdam became less safe for its Jewish residents. The relentless feeling of persecution and my longing for Philip became intolerable. I decided to take a chance and visit him one weekend. My friends did their best to dissuade me from traveling: the city was surrounded and no one could get through without being stopped at a checkpoint. But I refused to heed their warnings. The trip was certainly dangerous, but it was just as dangerous to stay in the city. Before setting out I made up a credible cover story. My plan succeeded and I made it to Laren and back to Amsterdam with no misadventure.

Grüne Polizei during razzia

That same weekend in June of 1943, Amsterdam suffered one of its largest raids.

Even the Althoff house was not spared.

Luckily I was not there when the notorious *Grüne Polizei* (Green Police) came to search the house. The hiding place (which would have been too small to hide me as well) proved its worth, and the Jewish family was not discovered. Saturday and Sunday passed very pleasantly for Philip and me, but the hours flew by and we were obliged to separate once more without knowing when we would see each other again.

Looking back, I know that I took impossible risks during the occupation. It was as if I was tempting fate and declaring: I'm not scared! Afterwards, it seemed to me I had been too reckless. For instance, I rode the electric tram even though this was forbidden to Jews. I did it just because of that!

A friend of my father caught sight of me on one of these trips and on the holy Sabbath too! Naturally, this friend felt he had to tell on me— the needless risk I had taken and the desecration of the Sabbath. After the war my brother Jaap (Jack) told me that when Father heard the story, he sank into deep thought and finally said enigmatically, "Maybe she's right after all." What a thoughtful answer my wise father gave his friend.

My sister Juul and her husband, Freddy, were arrested during the great Razzia (roundup). Using a spare key I went to their empty home on Sarphati Street a few days later. Petrified, I stared at a plate with leftovers of a fish meal on the kitchen table. The plates, the cutlery, the tablecloth and the bottle of wine bore mute testimony to the drama that had occurred there. The napkins were still there, thrown down in haste on the stained tablecloth. Only the kitchen clock continued ticking in the stillness. They were gone and I feared, forever.

As a final memento I took the fish forks and Juul 's housecoat, a tangible memory of the sister who was so violently taken

Jewish houses, whose owners had been deported, were emptied of their belongings. Everything that was deemed valuable was either shipped to Germany, sold or stolen. Prayer books, photo albums and letters were deemed 'worthless'.

from my life. Deeply saddened I left the house.

In this same period, on my way to the Central Station, I passed by the Gelderse Kade. Until then this street had been at the center of a vibrant Jewish neighborhood. I had to wade through heaps of torn pages from Jewish holy books, textbooks, letters, photo albums, kitchenware and other things the Germans, or perhaps greedy neighbors had thrown out. It was a confrontation with barbaric acts defiling an ancient culture.

My parents had many friends on Gelderse Kade and I wondered if perhaps some of the books and letters underfoot belonged to our own family. In silence I mourned my parents.

Despite their modern views they had adhered to religion and tradition: my mother, who worked outside the home before this was acceptable in society; my father who gave his daughters the freedom to play any sport they wished and who encouraged them to be independent thinkers. These parents, who wished their children to study, had been deported to

Westerbork transit camp, like refuse.

And there was no way to contact them. By visiting my brother and sister with my false identity I had already put myself in too much danger.

Thankfully, there was a possibility to send them packages. Sometimes friends of the Althoff family took them to the post office. Usually I prepared flat packages that fit in the postbox hanging at the back of the streetcar. They delivered them

Emptying the mail box at Amsterdam Central Station

straight at the Central Station's post office.

In spite of the tension we also had many lovely moments in the home of Eduard and Germaine Althoff. Germaine, who was born in Spain, gave private Spanish lessons. I became close friends with her two children, a boy and a girl, from a previous marriage. All kinds of artists frequently visited, and the house was often filled with music. In the midst of the desperate situation, we laughed a lot. But the laughter was cut short when, near the end of the war, the Germans shot and killed 36 Dutch citizens in the park opposite their house.

I had lived with them for barely two months when at three o'clock in the afternoon the doorbell rang. At that moment Germaine was teaching one of her private pupils. Two men wearing hats and raincoats, clearly secret police, stood at the bottom of the stairs. Instinctively I realized that we were in great danger. Hoping Germaine would hear me I shouted at the top of my voice,

"How can I help you, sirs?"

"You'll see as soon as we get upstairs!" they shouted back. Frightened, I ran to the study and whispered to Germaine, "Gestapo[1]! I only work here until five o'clock!" There were many stairs to the main floor. Full of trepidation I waited for the "guests" to arrive.

"Show your identity papers," the man in charge demanded. My identity card was a bad forgery, even the fingerprint didn't match. Only my picture and the note "scar on the right side of the neck" were genuine. A befriended doctor in Laren had painstakingly tattooed the scar on my neck and throughout the years of the war it looked very real and ugly. After the war the doctor made it vanish, without a trace.

While checking my identity papers they suddenly asked, "You have a scar? Show us!"

Feigning surprise I acted as if I had completely forgotten about the scar. "What? Is that written in my identity papers? How strange." Reluctantly I revealed the red scar on my neck. Masking my fear by chattering, I feigned to have remembered something. "Oh, I can't keep talking with you, I have to feed the baby!"

---

[1] The **Gestapo** ("Secret State Police"), led by Heinrich Himmler. It was considered a sister organization of the *Sicherheitsdienst* (SD) ("Security Service"). Anyone living in Nazi controlled territory lived in fear of a visit from the Gestapo.

"Who else is in the house?" they wanted to know.

"Mrs. Althoff is with a student. She is teaching Spanish."

"Tell her to come here," they demanded.

"What?" I exclaimed. "To disturb Mrs. Althoff when she's in the middle of teaching? Never! She has taken me on to take care of the baby and must not be disturbed while she's teaching. You will have to wait for her to finish at 5 p.m., or she will fire me!" I stood in front of her door like a guard dog.

As I had hoped, the men pushed me aside and entered the room. It gave me time to run upstairs to warn the Jewish family hiding in the attic.

"Gestapo! Hide!" I rushed to the baby's room, grabbed her out of bed and ran back to the kitchen. The frightened child, who had just fallen peacefully asleep on a full stomach, began to wail at the top of her voice.

After some time – the police were still in the living room with Germaine – I returned the baby to her bed. I put on a coat, took only my handbag, knocked on the door of the study, poked my head inside and said, "I'm going home now, Ma'am. It's 5 o'clock, my time to leave. See you tomorrow."

Germaine, who was in control of every situation, fell in with my acting. "Oh," she said in an annoyed tone of voice, "I hope you'll be on time for once. I'm tired of your constant tardiness."

"Yes Ma'am, I will. But I always have to wait so long for the tram." With all the self-confidence I could muster I walked down the stairs, closed the door behind me and disappeared. The Althoff family, who had become great friends, had to wait for my next visit until after the war.

Luckily this raid did not have disastrous consequences. The hiding place was not discovered. But the next day the Gestapo came back to the Althoff home. They had checked the identity of Jo Musch and what did they find out? That the nursemaid Mrs. Althoff innocently hired was a Jewess!

Mrs. Althoff managed to cry out, "Dear God, what danger I have been in. Oh, my poor baby!", and then fainted. Her credibility was impeccable.

That evening and night I wandered around Beatrix Park. Only the next morning did I dare travel to Huizen, a small village not far from Laren.

The home of the famous historians Jan and Annie Romein was always open to me. Known to be anti-Nazi, they conducted themselves with great discretion. Nevertheless, a year later Dr. Romein was taken into German detention.

Everyone who stayed in the Romein house knew that they had to be prepared to flee at a moment's notice. I slept in my clothes, a bag of essentials ready under the bed and an escape route prepared in advance.

Friends provided me with new identity papers, slightly better than the first ones, and this time with my own fingerprint. From now on my name would be Adrie Kool. Once again I practiced my new signature for hours, and committed the details of my new identity to memory. It was clear they were looking for me, and thus, as long as the occupation continued, I could not return to Amsterdam.

Adrie Kool laughed now and then, but Betty Polak rarely smiled anymore.

Liesje

"Camp" – what does that word mean? In September of 1943, when I was deported by train to Westerbork, this word acquired an entirely different meaning for me.

For years I had been going to the summer camps of the youth movement. At nighttime we slept in tents on hay-filled mattresses, happily chattering into the early hours of the morning.

It was the ideal summer vacation for us: two weeks sharing both happiness and youthful sorrow with the best of friends, and of course constantly falling in and out of love, far from our parents' watchful eyes. My first kiss, at age sixteen, was at summer camp.

The difference between the first camps in my life and the camp I found myself in at the age of twenty is almost indescribable.

In order to accommodate Jewish refugees from Germany, the Westerbork camp was established in 1939 by the Dutch Government. It was located near Assen, in the Province of Drenthe. After the German occupation the camp became a transit camp - a place to assemble the Jews of Holland before deporting them to the labor and death camps in Germany and Poland.

Westerbork was not the worst camp that existed in the territories conquered by the Nazis. It cannot be compared with the camps in Poland and Germany, notorious for their systematic murder of the Jews (of which we had not yet heard). But one thing was clear: our freedom had ended the moment we entered Westerbork. We had already lived in fear for so long, but in Westerbork while waiting for our turn on a transport list, it was difficult to entertain even the smallest ray of hope.

In their sinister wisdom the German lords placed the task of running the camp into the hands of its Jewish inmates. At our arrival at the camp we were received by very efficient Jewish administrators. After registration the newcomers were allocated barracks, men and women separately. Everything flowed smoothly and precisely. That entire first day at camp I did not see even one German. With amazing speed we became accustomed to our new fate. It was as if we had always lived like this – in a mass, with no privacy, no identity, our lives dictated by the rules of the camp.

We even became accustomed to "Damned Tuesday". I have often wondered how every week anew we managed to get through that awful night before Tuesday, the day a cattle train came to the so-called "*Boulevard des Misères*" - a newly built train station in the center of the camp. We all knew it had arrived to load human "cargo".

On Monday night the Jewish officials came into the barracks with the notorious lists and read out the names of those who were to leave the next day on the transport. These officials came as late as possible because they dreaded the reactions of those unfortunate people whose names were on the lists: the weeping of despair, the helpless scurrying hither and thither seeking desperately for a way out, the suicide attempts. The first to go were those who had just arrived, or who had not had time to settle in. If there weren't enough people, the veterans were taken. One could never know for sure who would be called and who would be spared on Tuesday, the day of judgment.

Some people had a kind of 'exemption'.

For various reasons they had managed to get onto a list that kept them, for the time being, off the deportation lists. Everyone tried to get a place on this list, even though they knew that it would only delay the inevitable. A long as the numbers tallied, the Germans did not care who was deported.

Usually it was 1,000 men, women and children, plus a few extras - people also died in the trains.

Since the Germans left the administration of the camp in the hands of the German and Austrian Jews a satanic situation was created: Jews had to push other Jews into the cattle cars. No one slept much on Monday nights. Those who were not to be transported did what they could to help the unfortunate ones pack their few belongings. We couldn't do much else than to support each other in sympathetic silence.

The train arrived on Tuesday morning and the people were shoved into the windowless, airless cattle cars. The buckets of water that were placed there would soon be empty; each car had one open barrel for human waste. The Germans counted the deportees one last time to make sure the numbers tallied, and bolted the heavy doors shut. And then the train began to roll away, painfully slowly, until it disappeared from view.

An eerie calm fell over the camp, a petrified silence. But we had to go on, and so we returned to our daily routines - until the next Tuesday.

In the camp I was reunited with my brother, Jaap (Jack), and my sister, Juul, who like me was physically not very strong. I saw them only rarely. They had their own troubles. To my sorrow I discovered that both their marriages had fallen apart.

My sister Betty was in hiding somewhere outside Amsterdam. Now and then we received letters, each time under a different name. She was obliged to change her identity again and again. These letters, which were always short, were a sign of life. They gave me joy, strength and allowed me to hope that one day we would meet again.

I was deeply grieved to learn that my parents had already been "sent on", in the language that had become common among the inhabitants of the camp.

"Father wrote you a goodbye letter", my brother told me, but I never saw the letter. The grief and longing has accompanied me my entire life. How I yearned to hold the letter my father had written me and to read his every word over and over again. What had my father wished to tell me in his last moments? I could guess. If he had written the letter on Friday, the Sabbath eve, he would have ended with the words, "May God bless you and protect you. Amen." He would have signed with his love, with endless blessings.

My father's deep faith always consoled me. Believing that God would protect us, his God deceived him. What did I really know about my parents, except for the fact that they were always there for me, like a constant, warm presence, one I took for granted. Who were they in their inner selves? What was the reason they were engaged for seven years before getting married? How did they endure the loss of their eldest son, a sweet blond boy who died of kidney disease at a very young age? How I would have liked to ask them of things that I hadn't thought of as a teen: what kind of childhood did they have, what were their own parents like? What did they think of life as they grew older, what did they expect of life?

I hadn't thought of these things, too engrossed with myself, as is the way with young people. And now, when I would so much like to know, there is no one to answer my questions.

Because I had been a second-year nursing student in the Jewish hospital in Amsterdam, I was put to work in Westerbork's large hospital barracks. There I met many of the doctors and specialists from the hospital, which had been transformed into a real hospital. It may be hard to believe, but a real surgery had been installed. The medication and medical equipment came from the outside. Even the sick were not excluded from the transports, and when beds became free on Tuesday they were quickly filled by new patients. Until the next transport they were cared for by the best Jewish doctors, who had been torn out of their beds, homes, places of work and sent to Westerbork. Each one of the doctors hoped, like the rest of us, to prove indispensable to the smooth running of the camp and be spared deportation. But this was a false hope. Even these prominent professionals disappeared one after the other. This endless fear! The uncertainty gnawing at our souls!

I lived in the same barracks as Ernst's mother and little sister. When the men were allowed to visit us for one hour in the evening, we shared our dinner. If one of us received a package, to our joy there would be extra food to go around.

I hardly saw Ernst and gradually our relationship began to change. We were not alienated, but the first bloom of our love withered and died before its time.

Perhaps it was life in the camp that killed our love, but it might have happened anyhow.

Most of the *halutzim* (pioneers) who had been about to leave for Palestine just before the war worked in the kitchen and the storeroom. Supervised by the SS, another group worked in the fields. I was the only one who worked in the hospital.

Perhaps because we didn't have families or children to look after, we felt responsible for each other.

Thanks to this indispensable support I was able to keep going in Westerbork.

Taking a stroll

In the meantime, life in the camp became harder and harder. There was not enough food. I was always hungry. But other things bothered me. My parents used to put great importance on moral values, which acted as a guide during my childhood. In the life that I knew people fell in love, were engaged, married and brought children into the world. As children, we never heard of scandals such as adultery or divorce.

Growing up in a puritanical environment, I now had to cope with a different reality of crowding and despair.

In Westerbork, life was lived moment by moment. In the camp I faced another side of life that shocked and bewildered me. Some people lived by the proverb: "Eat and drink, for tomorrow we may die" or "Enjoy life while you can and take all you can get!" Men and women had intimate relations with each other, regardless of whether it was with a stable partner or a chance encounter. They clung to a last moment of warmth and love.

In a dark corner of the camp I once caught sight of an older man - I knew him well; his wife was also in the camp. He intimately embraced a married distant relative of mine. As if drunk they kissed each other deeply, shamelessly.

I was stunned. How could they betray their spouses? But then I began to grasp a basic truth: these desperate people had no way of knowing whether they would even be alive next week!

Liesje's letter to Betty

Dearest Joke, (one of Betty's pseudonyms during the war),
We so enjoyed the good things you sent us, especially those wonderful apples! We don't get any of those here. I opened the package at dinner with Ernst's family and the whole family from The Hague. Everyone asked after you. It felt like St. Nicolas day, when we received all those packages! (A secular Dutch holiday where the family exchanges gifts.)
Recently five cases of polio have been discovered. The orphanage in Westerbork has been quarantined, no one is allowed in or out. They are terrified of an outbreak. The number of diphtheria cases is very high and hepatitis is spreading rampantly. It's hardly surprising: people are so crowded here that the danger of contagion is great. I am very lucky to be allowed to shower every week, thanks to my work. You get three minutes to take off your clothes, six minutes to shower and six minutes to get dressed again. I also wash myself every day, from head to toe, in ice-cold water.
As far as that is concerned, I have real privileges. If I make the effort, at noon I can also get hold of a mug of milk.

Despite the contagious diseases most probably another transport will be leaving this coming Tuesday. There have been rumors about a blue stamp that gives you an exemption. Anything is possible here in Westerbork. They say that we will be interned somewhere else. Whatever happens, we have to be patient and wait and see.
The hospital here doesn't look like a regular hospital anymore; it's like the sickbays we read about in books about the First World War. There are no sterile conditions.
Seriously ill people - over 100 of them - lie in a barracks with

bunk beds. Water is not easily accessible, only right up front in the washrooms. You have to go outside to get warm water. To bring a bedpan to a patient, you have to pass through the entire barracks. It is simply awful. Many people are suffering from diarrhea, the most common sickness here. I'm lucky not to have caught that yet.

The first day I couldn't bring myself to drink the water because it is so full of iron, but I've gotten used to it now. In any case, we don't drink a lot; otherwise we'd have to keep running to the toilet and to tell the truth, we don't actually get very thirsty. I always use the toilet at my work - thankfully a "real" toilet. You should see the "toilet shed" with space for 20 women having to sit next to one another – you can have a good gossip there – and the smell is awful.

And now it is five o'clock. I am the senior nurse in the department. A woman came in with her baby. She had mastitis (breast infection). After washing the baby, there was nothing to dress him with. I almost wept to see how neglected he was. His little behind was so red I couldn't bear to look at it. He hadn't had anything to drink since nine o'clock in the morning. I had no choice but to wrap him in a sheet and blanket. Hopefully this afternoon they'll bring diapers and clothes from another barracks. That's just one small example of what I experience at my work here. No supplies. No medication. No clothes.

My little great-niece, you know her - Greet's little daughter - had a sudden bowel obstruction and was so ill that she needed a blood transfusion. Her life is still in danger. Sadly, you become hardened here. Perhaps you have to be, otherwise you could cry all day.

Now it's Sunday evening. Greet's daughter died this morning. You can imagine what the family is feeling. So many children die here. The little children and the old people suffer the most. On Tuesday there is a transport. Those with the exemption stamp have the 'honor' of helping people onto the train, starting at three o'clock in the morning.

Yesterday I got another package from you, the one with the headscarf. I am so glad for it because I dread catching lice. Thank you again, from the bottom of my heart.
Besides that, yesterday another package arrived from my former employer, van der Weide. It was a big parcel with vegetables. You can't imagine how tasty they were, those carrots!!!
Try to let me know if you received this letter.
With all my love and best regards, you know who to.

Your Annie (a secret name for Liesje).

Betty

After a short stay with Jan and Annie Romein, I traveled to Den Haag as Adrie Kool. I got a job there as a maid in the anthroposophist home of the well known musician Han van Goudoever. There I had great luck: intelligent conversations, music and a special atmosphere. The couple helped me to take lessons in French and Russian. I was treated like one of the family. Only once I was scolded: when I wanted to throw away a withered bouquet. There I learned to recognize the beauty of wilted flowers.

Not being so sure I was a good maid, Philip once composed a poem in which he memorialized that Han had called me `a jewel`. When Han practiced Dvorak's cello concerto, I couldn't continue with the cleaning. With bated breath and my ears glued to the door, I listened to this heavenly music.

Alas, even the nice Benoordenhout, the beautiful quarter where the family lived, became a dangerous place. In that part of The Hague, the Germans started building the "Atlantic Wall", a defense along the western coast of Europe against a possible sea invasion. Because of the wall, the Germans began to barricade entire sections of the city. More and more checkpoints and barriers were erected.

We feared that they would tighten their surveillance of the areas within the barriers. And so, after three wonderful months, I was obliged to separate from those who had become like family to me.

Philip had left Laren a short while before. To our great joy, and thanks to my new connections, he was able to move to an open space – an anthroposophist horticultural farm in Groet, on the sea coast of North Holland. He felt right at home there. In his free time he thoroughly studied the theories of the anthroposophist Rudolf Steiner.

Every time I visited him I was deeply impressed with the special way people treated each other. In this relatively safe artist's village it was possible to visit other people freely. And so, in the short time Philip was at the village, we lived under the illusion of having returned to life in a 'normal' world.

The Goudoevers found a new job for me in Laren as a house-maid. I could not imagine a greater contrast between the place in The Hague where I was treated as a daughter and this new place in Laren. Arriving in the evening, I rang the door-bell of the enormous villa.

In all her glory the lady of the house opened the door and received me with the words, "So you're Adrie, the new maid."

She led me into the kitchen, my future domain. Passing by a narrow hall she pointed to the toilets, "That one is for you. Of course you understand you are not allowed to use ours." At that moment I realized what kind of a place I had landed in. My new employers expected me to appear on demand in a black dress with a white apron.

The next morning at 7 o'clock, even the little daughter put me in my place. "Oh, are you Adrie? Papa wants his breakfast now!" As I began to friendly say, "Good morning, Katinka", she responded arrogantly, "Do it right now, all right?"

Sadly I recalled the politeness with which my parents related to their house help and how they taught us to do the same. What a difference.

The lady of the house came rarely into the kitchen. Except on mornings when she received visitors, to prepare cocoa for her friends. Because cocoa was a rare commodity in war time I knew she was afraid I would take some of it for myself. With false gaiety she would say, "Adrie, you can have a cube of soup, all right?" She was referring to the unhealthy, salty soup substitute.

Special set for drinking hot chocolate

One evening my sister-in-law Suus, Philip's sister who was also hiding in Laren, visited me in the kitchen. Suddenly the lady entered, looked around for something and left just as quickly. Suus' face turned white. "That's L, we were in the same class in high school."

"Don't be afraid," I calmed her. "She didn't recognize you. As long as we do our work we are nothing more than air for her. If they do see us, it is only to order us around or to scold." The little girl had already taught me that much.

When some of us housemaids stood outside a villa gate waiting for the children to come out of a party or some other event, she always threw her coat on me and ordered, "Here, take it."

But the solidarity among the 'lower class' surprised me. When I asked the vegetable seller who came to our door how much a kilo of apples cost, I looked shocked when he told me the price.

Seeing my reaction, he put an arm around my shoulders and said, "Oh my dear, are they for you? Then it's half of that price."

Gradually I got used to my new name. When in a moment of inattention I left my bag with all my papers on the bus I needed another identity. It was too dangerous to go to the police to see if someone had found my bag. And so Adrie Kool became Ada Koole. The name had to be almost similar, as I was still in the same place of work.

In Laren I found people who were willing to send my little packages to family and friends in Westerbork. It would be dangerous to do it myself. One day the lady of the house was getting ready to go to the post office and I politely asked her if only once she was willing to send something for me. Finished with cleaning the big house, I returned to the kitchen and saw that my package was still on the kitchen table. At that same moment the lady came in, her arms full of packages and flowers. "Couldn't you take my package with you?" I asked, with difficulty restraining my anger.

"What did you think, Adrie? Surely you didn't expect me to mail my servant's packages?" the lady replied arrogantly.

It was the straw that broke the camel's back.

That same evening, when dinner went on until after nine o'clock and they called me back time and again to do silly demeaning tasks, I walked in to the dining room unasked and announced, "I am not staying in this house any longer. I quit tonight."

Everyone was shocked. "But whatever for?" the lady asked.

And then I loosened the rein from my tongue. "Why? Because for all your wealth and selfishness, you are not prepared to lift a little finger in aid of those who are dying of hunger in the concentration camps. For all your wealth, you are worth nothing! You only think of yourselves and your possessions."

The family tried to reason with me. They promised me everything, just so that I would stay. It seemed I was not such a bad maid after all. But nothing could persuade me to back down. I packed my things and left that same evening.

Once again I found myself enjoying the hospitality of Jan and Annie Romein. As I arrived at their place that same evening, Jan happened to celebrate his birthday. Still wearing my black dress and white apron I was received with joy.
As a birthday present I brought cocoa; no, I didn't steal it from 'the lady'. The tiny package had been with me ever since I had fled my home. I had guarded it carefully, and now the time had come to enjoy it with true friends.

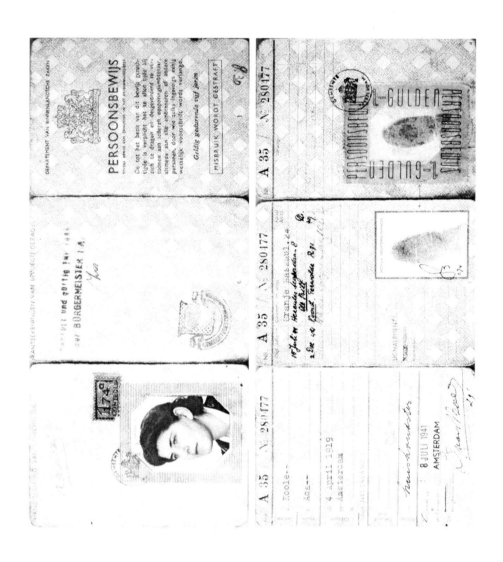

Betty's backdated false identity card. Ada Koole's occupation was listed as *huishoudster* (housekeeper)

Liesje

Valuable time was lost before the *Yishuv* (Jewish community in Palestine) began to realize what was happening to the Jews in Europe.

Between 1941 and 1942 Germans living in Palestine were exchanged with the few lucky ones who had immigration certificates for Palestine, or who held Palestinian citizenship and for some reason had been caught up in the war in Europe. When they arrived in Palestine in 1942 and began to speak of what they had seen and experienced, for the first time the Palestinian Jews became aware that death camps had been erected for the extermination of their brethren. Time was of the essence to save as many Jews as possible from the valley of death in the occupied countries. However, only those with valid immigration papers to Palestine, stamped by the British Mandate authorities, were permitted to enter the land. In order to control the numbers of Jews entering the Promised Land the British had begun to issue immigration papers as early as the 1930s. Despite the war, the pro-Arab, anti-Zionist British government not only refused to alter their stance, but even tightened their restrictions. The authorities refused to provide papers to Jews living in countries conquered by the enemy.

In Holland, efforts were made to enable emigration for those who had received valid Palestinian immigration papers even before the war. In this connection the *Joodsche Raad* published a notice in *Het Israelitische Weekblad* (a Jewish weekly newspaper) on October 30, 1942. This notice, as it appears below, was published at the height of the deportations which had begun several months earlier.

The Department of Immigration of the Joodsche Raad in Amsterdam announces that:

1. People who held immigration certificates for Palestine before the war,
2. Small children whose parents live in Palestine,
3. Parents whose children live in Palestine and who hold certificates, or confirmation of their eligibility for a certificate,

may present themselves at the Joodsche Raad Department of Immigration, 336 Lijnbaansgracht. They must provide personal details and the address of their parents/children in Palestine, and a short description of the circumstances in which their relatives immigrated to Palestine (date, profession and so on).

Any application made by persons who do not belong to one of these three groups will not be considered.

In order to avoid raising false hopes, we wish to reiterate that this is only for the purpose of a preliminary registration. This does not guarantee immigration to Palestine.

We request that the details above be written by hand, as soon as possible. If necessary, notification will be given of the date for a personal interview.

Dutch Jews living in Palestine established an Action Committee which prepared lists of names of their relatives in Holland. Naturally, each one listed as many names as he possibly could, not only of his relatives but also friends and acquaintances. These lists were submitted to the Mandate authorities with the urgent request to provide these people with certificates so that if the exchange occurred, they could be delivered from the claws of the Nazis. Everyone knew with certainty that papers had to be produced, whether real or forged, as quickly as possible.

COMITÉ INTERNATIONAL DE LA CROIX-ROUGE

GENÈVE (Suisse) Service Hollandais

FD/mk

DEMANDEUR — ANFRAGESTELLER — ENQUIRER

Nom - *Name* .... JEWISH AGENCY

Prénom — *Vorname — Christian name* ....

...e - *Strasse - Street* ....

Localité - *Ortschaft - Locality* .... JERUSALEM

Département - *Provinz - County* ....

Pays - *Land - Country* .... Palestine

Message à transmettre — Mitteilung — Message

(25 mots au maximum, nouvelles de caractère strictement personnel et familial)—
*(nicht über 25 Worte, nur persönliche Familiennachrichten) – (not over 25 words,
family news of strictly personal character).*

Message du 14.10.43 pour M.Elisabeth Alida POLAK &
fam... Camp Westerbork, Barr.69. HOOGHALEN, Drente

"Vous êtes enregistrés sur la IVe liste des
Vétérans Sionistes". Votre No.est

m/438/43/d/49

Date - *Datum* .... 18.10.4[3]

DESTINATAIRE — EMPFÄNGER — ADDRESSEE

Nom - *Name* .... JOODSCHE RAAD

Prénom - *Vorname - Christian name* ....

Rue - *Strasse - Street* .... Lijnbaansgracht 366

Localité - *Ortschaft - Locality* .... AMSTERDAM

Province - *Provinz - County* ....

Pays - *Land - Country* .... Hollande

RÉPONSE AU VERSO	ANTWORT UMSEITIG	REPLY OVERLEAF
Prière d'écrire très lisiblement	Bitte sehr deutlich schreiben	Please write very clearly

Palestine Certificate for Liesje, October 18, 1943

Chaim Pazner and his wife oversaw the production of certificates and letters of eligibility from their Palestine Office in Geneva. They believed that everything possible had to be done to save Jewish lives. When details in the lists – there were six lists totaling 1,892 names – were incomplete, couriers were smuggled into Europe to obtain the missing details. It was a dangerous mission. Contacting people within occupied countries by letter was only possible through the Red Cross.

They issued special forms with a maximum of 25 words. The receipt of a certificate was also notified by the Red Cross.

The Pazners knew it was impossible to wait for the official numbering of certificates -- every minute counted. Thus they established their own numbering system.

"The most important thing," they argued, "is that the certificate has a number."

We received our certificates in Westerbork; for many of them it came too late. My parents and I were on the second list of those who were eligible, but before obtaining the long awaited papers my parents had been already murdered in the gas chambers of the Sobibor extermination camp in Poland.

The Germans must have known that many of the certificates were forged, but that did not interest them. They simply wanted to retain a 'reserve group' who could, if necessary, be exchanged for Germans trapped behind enemy lines.

This 'reserve group' was not deported to the death camps, but to the Bergen-Belsen transit camp, from where exchange deals went out. We hoped it would be Bergen-Belsen and not Sobibor or Auschwitz, where people were sent in cattle cars.

None of us could imagine that in Bergen-Belsen too, thousands would die of starvation, exhaustion and infectious diseases.

The rumor spread within Westerbork: the SS sent Fraulein Gertrude Schlottke[1] to the camp in order to select people for the exchange to Palestine from among those on the list.

I prayed that she would be my salvation - that I would never again have to go through those terrible Tuesdays.

People in the camp warned me, "If Fraulein Schlottke sends for you and asks where your parents are, by no means say that they have been sent East. You must tell her in your best German that your parents died when you were very young and that you came to Westerbork with your fiancé's family, and you belong to them. Otherwise Fraulein Schlottke will put you on the deportation list, because her motto is, "We want to keep families together, so we will send you to join your parents.""

This warning saved my life. Luckily it was not too difficult to convince her who I belonged to. Ernst and I had registered for marriage in the Amsterdam city hall even before we came to Westerbork. We had hoped they would not separate a married couple.

The camp was uneasy, there were always rumors - sometimes good ones, sometimes evil ones. This time, it was whispered that those holding Palestine certificates would soon be transferred to the Bergen-Belsen transit camp in northern Germany. For once, the rumor of good tidings proved to be true.

---

[1] Ms. Schlottke was the secretary of Hanns Albin Rauter, the highest SS police leader during the war. He reported directly to SS chief Heinrich Himmler and to the Nazi governor of Holland: Arthur Seyss-Inquart.

BERGEN-BELSEN

Letter from Liesje to Betty

Westerbork, January, 1944

Dear Adrie,

It is Monday night, ten minutes before midnight. This is the last of several letters I have sent you recently. Most of them never reached you.

I have so much to tell you, and I always want to share with you what is happening in my life. By the way, do you know how many people come up to me to say how much I look like my sister?

Life here is very hard, and a lot has happened lately. I don't know where to begin.

Tomorrow Liesje will travel to Bergen-Belsen, near Celle, close to Hannover. That is a detention camp. The travelers are allowed to take their belongings with them. They are going in a passenger train! We will be able to receive mail, so you can write if you wish.

How very different this trip is from the transports to Auschwitz. Last week another 1,000 people were carried off in cattle cars. Why the difference? Freddy and his wife left for Celle three weeks ago. Trude, Bobby and others got a postponement because Jacques was very ill. Sadly, he died last week. You cannot imagine how hard it hit us and how unbelievably brave everyone was. Those are the facts of life here and we have to deal with them...

No one is sorry to leave this place, not even Liesje. We have had more than enough trouble. Life here is foul, rotten and dirty. And yet, we have come to know good people who taught us lessons for life. How I long for a decent bed – with lots of blankets and real sheets and a pillow for my head.

It's not that I'm complaining; I'm not. I am deeply grateful for my two blankets and sleeping bag, and my bread sack under my head. Sometimes I miss the small things terribly, but you get used to anything. I wish I could be alone for a while, but that is impossible: there are always people, and more people. The only privacy you get is the five minutes in the weekly shower. You can imagine how much we enjoy that. Since we can't receive packages anymore food is the biggest problem. It isn't easy to be hungry. I have been lucky not to have suffered real hunger until now. I am trying to get used to it.

But this week I wept in anger when they wouldn't give me a fresh carrot in the hospital. Would you ever have thought that a carrot would be a reason to cry? What has become of us?

But you mustn't worry. I'm just writing how things really are, and even though it doesn't sound nice, we are managing. All of us have aged.

I had an infection on my thumb. Under general anesthesia they had to make a deep cut, because the infection caused blood poisoning in my arm up to my armpit. And then I got erysipelas and a fever of over 104 ^{0}F (40 ^{0}C) for several days. But the medical care was excellent! I still can't use the tip of my thumb, but I managed to put it all behind me.

Jaap (Jack) and Manja received certificates and will be traveling to Celle in three weeks. Betty and her husband also have certificates; they are on the fifth list.

It is almost the middle of the night now. I am sleeping on the third bunk in the middle of the barracks. The place looks like a second-hand clothing store. All the things that are kept on the bed during the day are hanging from the ceiling beams now. It is never quiet here, there is the endless crying of children and people constantly going to or returning from the washhouse. I have pretty much all the clothes I need.

I would, of course, gladly add a dress or long pants, but besides that I have everything. Here you learn to share and help each other as much as possible. You can even enjoy yourself if you wish to. The sunrise and sunset can be so beautiful. And it is a pleasure to listen to Bé (Beatrix) Pimentel playing the piano. We are satisfied with so little. Could I have imagined that life would be so difficult? No, and I would rather never have known. On the other hand, if I survive, I will have learned something valuable for life. I just have to get through it. But still, I am optimistic. I only worry about the after-effects that someday in the future will come. The worst of it is that our family will have to face its biggest problems after the war.

First, we will look for mother and father, and then Jaap (Jack) will get a divorce. Freddy also wants a divorce but Juul will never agree to it [1]. We are setting off in another half an hour. I am sitting on my bed amongst all my belongings. For your ears alone: I find it hard to leave. I hope that we will meet soon, very soon! A big hug, and wishing you all the very best, Your L.

---

[1] The eight-year difference made it difficult for Liesje to talk about difficulties with Juul. Everyone tried to survive and stay out of the clutches of the Nazis. A week after liberation from Bergen-Belsen Juul died of starvation and typhus. Knowing her marriage was over probably didn't give her the will to live. Despite the many years that have passed, Liesje still grieves she was unable to help her sister the way she did patients under her care.

In January 1944 we left Westerbork. We, the "chosen ones", had to travel by regular train, not a cattle train, which was already a good omen. Of course we were to be closely guarded, locked behind bolted doors; still, hope filled my heart.

After having been through so much, could anything worse happen to me now?

Shouting, raging Nazi soldiers with large, fierce guard dogs were waiting for us at Bergen-Belsen. After a decent, 'human' train ride we arrived in hell. This, we soon realized, was not Westerbork. Men were separated from women and children, our belongings loaded onto another large truck – this is how we entered the camp. Dejected and fearful we looked around us. Jews from all over Europe were gathered in the same place – the Hungarian Jews were brought to a camp of their own. There were Russian prisoners of war. We heard whispers in every language imaginable, like the confusion of the Tower of Babel all over again.

As we were marched to our camp we passed men standing close to the fence. It must have been a long time since they had seen a woman. Their hungry stares aroused pity and aversion at the same time.

We were quickly divided into work detail.

As luck would have it, our friends from the *hachshara* were again sent to work in the kitchen; I was sent to the "Revier", the clinic.

Barracks Bergen Belsen (1945)

Roll-call was twice a day, standing five in a row, rain or shine. We were counted. If the numbers didn't tally, the counting began all over again from the beginning. Sometimes we stood there for hours, even the sick ones among us, and many fell ill from the cold winds and rain.

The "toilets" were outdoors – long, narrow shacks with holes in the floor and no partitions. Even those of us who had become used to it at Westerbork were appalled. The bunks were stacked three stories high, and I slept on the top next to a friend. The straw mattresses we had to fill ourselves reminded me of the camp of my youth. I happened to have a blanket that someone in Westerbork had given as a goodbye present.

Everything I owned was stored on the small bed. My rucksack, which served as a pillow; the blanket to protect me from the cold winter nights; the few clothes I had stuffed into my rucksack and my purse. My name and birth date I embroidered in large letters on the blanket because stealing was rife. A stolen piece of clothing may one day turn up, but a carefully hidden piece of bread, once gone, was lost forever. Our lives centered on food and the struggle for survival.

In my purse I kept my most precious possessions: photos, including one of myself with the van der Weide family in Sloten, already wearing the yellow star. How free I had felt among these kind friends. I had no mementos of my parents other than my mother's small sewing scissors. I still have it, and use them every day.

At 12 o'clock noon the women in the camp would sit down at the long table in the barracks. "Lunch" was soup which consisted of anything and everything that could be cooked and was served in a large metal kettle. It was a lukewarm liquid with kohlrabi and sometimes a piece of pork. The soup was first served to the elderly and the children. Then it was the turn of the working women, who fell hungrily upon the miserable concoction.

An hour later the women were beckoned to roll-call yet again, and then returned to work. I usually ate in the hospital barracks, but one day before my shift began I stayed to eat lunch with the women in my barracks. I watched them.

What a depressing sight! I had known some of them in Amsterdam. Their faces, aged and paled, had become lifeless. Their eyes were expressionless and sunken deep into their sockets. They were mere shadows of their former selves. We young people had a purpose that kept our hopes up. We belonged to the Zionist movement, supported each other and declared with determination: "After the war up to Palestine!"

The terrible living conditions brought down any past barriers between the orthodox and secular members of the Zionist youth movements. Most of us had already lost our families (even though we did not always know it for sure, the constant worry for our loved ones ate away at us). We were alone, and if we hadn't stuck together and cared for each other, we would have sunk into despair. The feeling of responsibility for one another turned us into one family.

Former members of the *hachshara* risked their lives to "organize" food for those who did not have the luck of working in the kitchen.

Being constantly hungry, I developed my own strategy. After observing the distribution of the food I noticed that each kettle contained about 25 portions of soup. I maneuvered myself into the 20th place in line for I knew that the actual pieces of food, if any, sank to the bottom of the pot.

Where – in God's name – did I learn to be so coldly calculating? The desperate desire to survive changed me.

It brought up something that was not a natural part of my character.

```
                    A u s w e i s.

        POLAK,       Elisabeth

        geb.am:      4. 2.22
        ist als Schwester

        im Revier eingestellt.

               Bergen-Belsen,den 25.3.44.

                         Der Lagerarzt.
                         i.V.
        S.S.Oscha.            S.S.Uscha.
```

Permit stating Liesje works at the 'hospital' (Revier)

A Night in Bergen-Belsen

I had the night shift. Holding a small flashlight I carefully walked through the pitch black of the camp to the hospital barracks. The nurse from the evening shift sat bowed over the table. In the weak light of one small bulb I saw she looked tired.

"Nothing special," she reported. "Five patients will not survive the night."

Nothing special! Just the usual routine. Five would join the cycle of death tonight. Maybe more - seven, ten. Who would they be? Children? Women? Men? I could hear their groans. Some were too weak to even moan.

"Good night," I said, and the nurse went to rest after an exhausting day of work.

Before the war, I would not have begun a shift without carefully going over the pages of medical reports, or checking the medication trolley. But now, who thought of such things? There was no paper, let alone medications. The only way to provide some solace to the deadly ill was to hold their hand, stroke them, hug them, rearrange their straw mattress and give them an encouraging word. The only medication to be offered was a sip of water from the single tap in the hut.

So many died quietly, without a fuss. When someone died, we had to leave him in his bed until morning light, and then the body was taken away. Their places were quickly filled by others.

I walked along the rows of beds. Gently I stroked the forehead of the sleeping Dr. P. Yesterday I sat by his bed, holding his hand as he talked non-stop for over two hours. It was a strange feeling. This doctor of renown had never revealed his feelings to anyone the way he did to me, a 20-year old stranger. I wondered what more I could do to help him, how I could give him the strength to continue living?

He told me of his youth in Germany, of his work as a doctor in Holland, of his sons. He knew his days were numbered. There was no medicine for him. I had nothing to give him other than my patience and willingness to listen. When he reached the end of his memories, I felt I had helped him. I could see it in his eyes.

Gideon, just sixteen years old, was no longer able to stand on his feet. Before I sat down at my table, I walked over to him. He knew I was on the night shift. A joyful smile spread over his pale face. "Hello Nurse, I have been waiting for you." Not asking how he was, I hugged him gently and carefully.

"Are we traveling anywhere tonight?" he asked.

"Of course", I answered, "I have the tickets ready!"

This was our game. We "traveled" together to Paris, to London, visiting museums, studying the works of famous artists. Everything I remembered from high school I shared with this young boy. He had not been able to go to a regular school, and now, in the face of death, he thirstily drank in all the culture he could get.

"Gideon", I told him, "Today I have a special surprise for you. I have air tickets and we are flying to a warm country, to the south of Spain, and we'll be able to lie on the beach in the sun. That will make you better."

"But I'm afraid of flying," he interrupted me.

"Don't worry, I'll be with you. Just hold my hand and close your eyes. We have gone through passport control. We got great seats. You're next to the window. Now we will sit down and put on our seatbelts. Hold my hand tightly!"

He clung to me with the little bit of strength he had left. We flew high up in the sky to the clouds and higher, to eternity. I felt his grip slowly loosening. He had fallen asleep.

"Good night, my angel, I hope you don't suffer too much," I murmured, stroking his head.

I sat down at the table. The light above my head was very dim. I was afraid of the darkness. One day during the afternoon shift a schizophrenic young girl crept out of her bed and attacked me from behind. Grabbing my hair with both hands she yanked me back with all her might. None of the patients could help me. Fortunately for me, a passerby heard my cries. He rushed inside, and whipped the patient's hands with his belt until she let go. For months I suffered dreadful headaches. Since that traumatic experience I was afraid to be left alone with this girl. She was very pretty and looked quite normal, but we never knew when she would have one of her fits. We wondered if we would be able to keep her on as a patient, and for how long we could hide her mental illness from the Germans.

A 'squeezer flashlight'

Once again I made the rounds to see if anyone needed a drink. A sip of water was all I could give them. Suddenly the solitary light bulb burned out. The little 'squeezer' flashlight I always carried with me helped me to find my way back to the chair.

To cope with my fear of the dark, I conjured up a concert hall with an orchestra, a conductor and soloists, including an enthusiastic audience. Music had been one of the most important things in my life. Since the age of twelve I visited the major concerts in Amsterdam. Now I improvised the music in my head: Mozart's 40th symphony, then Beethoven's fifth. My concert concluded with Vivaldi's Four Seasons – the soft, hopeful strains of "Spring".

Outside a dog barked. Night inspection was coming.

The door opened and a young, heavy-set German entered. The large flashlight blinded me. "Anything to report?"

"No, Sergeant", I answered. "All is well."

He shone the beam around until it fell on me. "Oh, is it you Liesje?" he said.

Everyone knew me. I was young, always made a point of smiling, spoke fluent German.

"Yes, it's me Sergeant."

The German took a candle out of his pocket, lit it with a match and stuck it on my table. "That's better", he said, and left the hut without another word.

I warmed my frozen hands in the heat of the flickering candle. The night came to an end; entering quietly the stretcher bearers took care of their painful task.

The morning shift nurses arrived and I left. As the hospital was located in the men's' camp, I had permission to be there. They had left in the early hours of the morning and now the camp was quiet and empty. I was lucky to be able to sleep here, rather than in the women's barracks with the constant noise of children. Here I could enjoy absolute silence.

I climbed up to my fiancé's bunk, read the note he had left before going out to work and fell asleep immediately.

Another typical night, one of many at Bergen-Belsen.

Drawing by Louis Asscher

Liesje

The moment we arrived in Bergen-Belsen we no longer felt safe. Although we knew that our certificates were our only chance to evade our fate, who could assure us of that? In the new camp we were taken up by the daily struggle for survival and quickly forgot we were 'privileged'. Day followed day, and nothing happened. Had our hope only been an illusion? People were sent from Bergen-Belsen to Auschwitz or Sobibor, not to freedom.

And then the day came in June, 1944, when the First Sergeant read out a list of names, mine among them. We had half an hour to pack our belongings and move to another barrack. There we were told: "You're going to Palestine." We couldn't take it in, wondering if this could really be true.
Our entire group – 200 people - headed for Palestine as part of the Templar exchange.

In the 19th century a devout group of Lutherans from Stuttgart left Germany for Palestine. The "Templars" as they were called, established flourishing agricultural settlements in the land, and picturesque neighborhoods in the larger cities. Despite the distance, they remained German at heart. When Hitler rose to power, many of the Templar men returned to Germany to fight in the army, leaving their wives and children behind in Palestine. When war broke out, the British authorities interned the Templar families in a camp at Atlit, south of Haifa. After some time the Templars in Germany pressured their Nazi government to restore their families to their "home in the Reich".

After the first exchange more bargaining followed to equal the numbers of Jews and Germans in a subsequent swap which was to take place in July 1944. In this way, 222 Jews were rescued from Bergen-Belsen. I was one of them.

I do not know who approved the final list of the exchange. Only much later did I understand why one day, while working in the Jewish hospital in Amsterdam, a stranger had asked me for my full name and birth date. Neither Ernst and his family, nor my brother Jaap (Jack) and Manja, nor my sister Juul and Freddy, nor any of my dear friends were on the list. Only my name appeared on it.

The people of our group were mostly older people who did not have much longer to live, and a few families with small children. And seven young women who had to make sure everyone arrived in Palestine alive and whole, as had been agreed to. Those seven had been chosen out of hundreds possessing Palestine papers. I realized that my choice of a nursing career had, without a doubt, saved my life.

The new barrack was divided into a department for women and men. We didn't have to work, and there was only one roll-call a day. The food was brought here in the same big metal kettles. By way of notes, stuck in the kettle, we kept in touch with our friends and families. The seven totally different, unmarried girls stuck close together. One warm evening we sat outside the barrack, singing a canon, "how pleasant the evening is when the bells ring in the quiet." When our song ended a soldier called from the watchtower, "Please, sing it again!" I often wondered how the soldier felt at the time.

After about two weeks, when we were becoming accustomed to the peace and quiet, we were dragged out of our beds in the middle of the night for roll-call. Fifty names were called out. These people were ordered to step out of the line, pack their belongings and had to go back to their former barracks. Much later we heard the reason why: another detention camp in Vittel, France, held many people with certificates for Palestine. These could join our group in Vienna, on condition that 50 names be struck from our list. Only a few of those who were sent back to their former barracks survived the war.

Sometime later it was announced, "You are leaving for Palestine tomorrow. At seven in the morning you must be outside with your belongings, ready to go."

That night we were too excited to sleep. The constant sound of planes flying over our heads added to the tension in the air. From time to time we heard sirens and the distant sound of bombing. Surely the British wouldn't bomb the camp tonight, of all nights?

The next day at seven o'clock we waited at the gate with our belongings. In vain.

"The trip has been postponed indefinitely," we were told. The train tracks had been bombed. We were obliged to return to our former barracks. It was hard to believe, but I was glad to be back, to stay with my family and my friends who I did not want to leave.

But Ernst and many others convinced me with, "No, you must get out of here now. Maybe from the outside you will be able to help and save us."

They prepared a list of names and addresses of Dutch Resistance members. I had to inform them about what was happening and ask for their urgent help.

Several weeks went by. We had already forgotten about our certificates when one night we were woken up and ordered to gather outside the main building in one hour. We were allowed to bring only our clothes.

It was a quiet summer night; no bombings. In my rucksack I packed a few clothes; in my purse I stuffed everything that was most precious to me – a few photos, my mother's sewing scissors and the list with Resistance members.

Seeing how thoroughly the Germans searched our bags, I looked for a way to slip my bag through unnoticed. The tables were piled high with bags. After passing inspection, they were marked with a white chalk cross. The sergeant I knew from the daily inspection at the gate of the men's camp stood next to one table. I met him every day on my way to the hospital, and each time he greeted me with a smile and the words, "Good morning, Liesje."

This time he also greeted me. Smiling at him I stealthily picked up a piece of chalk and drew a white cross on my handbag. When my turn for inspection came, I quickly shoved the handbag away to the other side of the able, as if it belonged to the person in front of me, sticking my rucksack under the nose of the SS guard.

After passing safely through inspection, we were allowed to take our belongings from the pile. A stone fell from my heart: the lists and my small collection of mementos had been saved.

We marched to Celle train station, a distance of some twenty kilometers. Those who were too weak to walk were taken by truck. It was midnight.

Sadly, we had not been allowed to say our goodbyes.

I had been saved, but what was going to happen to all those left behind?

At the empty station we were each given a chunk of bread and a sausage for the way. After all those months of watery soup, this was like angel food to us.

In our group there was a family with four children. Their eldest son, 16 years old, was dying of advanced tuberculosis. I knew him from the hospital. His parents faced a terrible dilemma: should they leave him behind in the camp and save the rest of the family, or give up their chance of rescue and stay with him in the camp? The parents cherished the small hope that if he survived the long journey, he would receive the necessary medical care in Palestine. It was none other than the SS doctor himself who decided for them by saying,

"Take him. Here he won't last long, but perhaps over there, they will be able to save him."

The deathly-ill boy was brought to the train station on a stretcher. We prepared a bed for him the best we could. Innumerable times I checked on him, to see if he was still breathing! We couldn't believe what was happening to us, traveling on a real train with seats and windows, on our way to freedom. True, the doors were bolted, but no German soldier was could be found in the carriages. When the train stopped at a station, the soldiers stood quietly, smoking a cigarette and chatting with each other, not paying us any attention at all. There was more than enough room in the train carriages. At night we slept on the benches. Some carriages even had benches that opened up into beds. These were given to the oldest and weakest among us. The few small children were put to bed on the luggage stands. Traveling through Nazi Germany, from time to time the train was forced to stop until the rubble from previous bombings could be cleared from the tracks.

The first days we sat in silence, each of us occupied with his own thoughts. We gazed out of the window in wonder, speechless. In places that had not been bombed, life seemed to go on as usual. Everywhere flowers bloomed, cows grazed peacefully in green meadows, and we could hear the birds chirping. Was this the same world that fought against us, that had abandoned us? Slowly we drew closer to each other, but didn't speak of what we had left behind. A silence fell over that period, we spoke only what life was like in Palestine, and what ours would be like over there.

We travelled through Munich, arriving one afternoon in Vienna. Buses were waiting to take us to a large building several stories high – a refuge for the homeless. On the top floor we were received by officials from the Red Cross. Until that moment we had not dared to fully believe in our final destination. Were we really being taken to Palestine, or with typical deceit were the Nazis transporting us to an extermination camp?

The Red Cross officials who were awaiting us dissipated our fears. Dear God, we were free! Our dream had come true.

We were given a warm meal and a bed with clean sheets and a pillow. Restless, I could only think of the request to let the Dutch Resistance know of the threatening situation. Obtaining a pen and paper, I began to write many carefully worded letters which had to pass the eyes of the censor.

My next problem was how to mail them?

In my uniform, but without the yellow star, I pretended to be a nurse working with the Red Cross. Once outside on the unfamiliar street, I had the wonderful experience of being able to walk freely, and in the most beautiful town I had ever seen. Using my most polished German I asked a young man where I could find a post office. He answered, "The post office is already closed." As we talked, he told me that he was a Czech working as a builder in Vienna.

"I'm only in Vienna for a very short time, and don't have a chance to send my letters," I told him. "Could you do me a favor and mail them for me?"

The kitchen workers in Bergen-Belsen received a monthly ration of cigarettes and Ernst had given me some 'in case of emergency'. In lieu of money, cigarettes were a prime bartering commodity. To pay for the stamps I gave the Czech worker all the German coins I possessed, and added a few cigarettes.

All the letters reached Holland. They couldn't save the Jews in Bergen-Belsen, but now they had an eye-witness account to what was happening. And in this way, Betty also learned that her little sister was on her way to Palestine!

As I returned to the building, I witnessed the arrival of two large trucks crowded with men, women and children, all wearing yellow stars. Shouting German soldiers drove them from the trucks into the courtyard. Under Eichmann's most recent initiative these Hungarian Jews were sent to Auschwitz. Terrified, shocked, sobbing with fear, these people huddled together. They were well dressed, carrying bags and suitcases as if they were going on a pleasure trip. Throughout the war years they had not believed the news filtering through from the occupied European countries. Now evil had overtaken them.

I stood there, horrified, as if my feet had turned to stone. What could I, Liesje Polak, do for them? Praying for a miracle I threw the little bread I had left from my journey into the open truck. In the courtyard the Hungarian Jews, on their way to imprisonment and death were heavily guarded by the SS. We, on the top floor under the protection of the Red Cross, were on our way to freedom and to life.

The next day we continued our journey.

After crossing the Hungarian border when the train was on the outskirts of Budapest we learned that the train station had been bombed and completely destroyed. After several delays and accompanied by the sound of constant air raid sirens, we eventually reached Bulgaria. It was exciting to see mountains for the first time in my life. It had been such a long time to be in a well-lit and undestroyed city. Thanks to the stand of King Boris, the church and the population, Bulgaria was the only European country whose 50,000-strong Jewish community survived the Nazi terror.

The closer we drew to our destination, the more the sick boy's will to reach Palestine alive intensified. He would lie longer with his eyes open; also his breathing became deeper and easier.[1]

It was a beautiful Wednesday morning, the 7th of July, 1944. Eight days had passed since we left Bergen-Belsen and we had traveled through four countries before finally crossing the Turkish border. Now we were on our way to Istanbul.

Representatives of the Red Cross as well as Turkish and Swiss diplomats met us at the train station. Visibly shocked by our gaunt and feeble appearance, they took us straight to the cruise ship that sailed the River Bosporus. We crossed the strait, but when we reached the other side the boat turned about and returned the way it had come. To our astonishment this maneuver happened again and again! We didn't understand what was going on. It may be very pleasant to ride the waves of the Bosporus, but surely we had not undertaken such an arduous journey to sail in a cruise ship and gaze upon the mosques and the blue sea of Istanbul.

---

[1] Upon arrival in Palestine he was taken directly to a Tuberculosis sanatorium in the Safed hills, where he stayed for a very long period. In the end, the impossible happened - he was released with a clean bill of health.

Years later we learned about the many mishaps of those hours. The exchange was to have taken place in the middle of the Bosporus. However, the number of Jews arriving from Bergen-Belsen was greater than the number of Templars from Palestine.

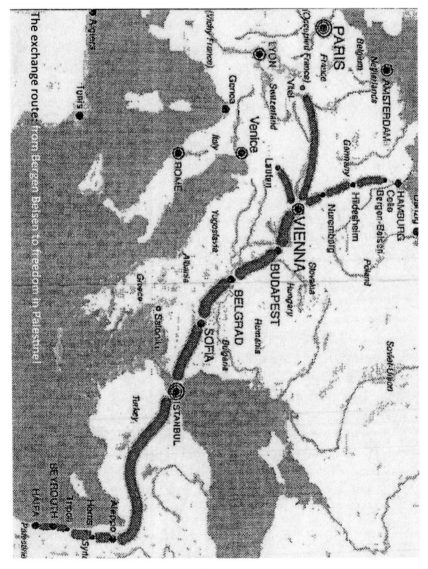

The exchange route: from Bergen Belsen to freedom in Palestine!

The negotiations had dragged on over several hours. Furthermore, the Templars[1] (for the most part women and children whom we never laid eyes upon), had arrived late. All these details held up the exchange. It was only towards evening that the green light was given to finalize the matter.

Once we had permission to disembark at the Bosporus pier, we boarded a train under the protection of British soldiers who were to accompany us to Palestine. The soldiers did their best to make us comfortable on the last leg of our journey, and offered us a sumptuous supper with omelet. Most regrettably, our stomachs revolted immediately. Not one of us was able to digest a normal meal.

Slowly the train followed the Turkish coast, and then south through Syria and Lebanon. The expansive Mediterranean coastline was exquisite. We passed under white cliffs, and through a tunnel with an Arabic sign, "*Ras el Nakura*", Rosh HaNikra, now the northernmost point of the coast of Israel.

"You're in Palestine," the soldiers announced.

Moved to tears, we all stood up as one, and sang the Jewish anthem, *HaTikva*. In truth, we wept more than we sang.

Watching the arrival of the prisoners from the camps in Europe no one remained dry-eyed. All the way to Haifa people gathered along the railway tracks, welcoming their brothers and sisters. While the train slowly passed they threw flowers and fruit through the open windows.

We couldn't stay in Haifa. For fear that we may be bearing infectious diseases, we were taken to quarantine at Atlit. Ironically, before their exchange the Templar women had been held in this camp as well.

Safely "home", my dream had finally come true.

---

[1] On their way home the Templar women received a euphoric hero's welcome at every train station they passed in Germany. Upon arrival in Stuttgart they were caught in the British bombardment of the city.

HIDING TOGETHER

Betty

In the summer of 1944, Philip and I found a hiding place with an artist couple blessed with many children who lived in Lage Vuursche, a small village in central Holland. Their house was large and roomy, set in the middle of an extensive yard used to grow vegetables.

Philip and I were accommodated in the old chicken coop. I worked in the house and Philip on the farm. It wasn't ideal, but at least we were together. Despite the fact that we worked hard, they charged so much for our 'room' and board that I was obliged to sell my last pieces of jewelry.

I was terribly worried about Liesje, who had been transported from Westerbork to Bergen-Belsen, and even more for my parents. We had not received any sign of life from them for quite some time.

The wonderful forests and expansive open spaces around Lage Vuursche could not ease my worried state of mind. The lady of the house was bad-tempered and hard to please. One day she shouted at me, "I have never seen you laughing! Something had better change!" Completely taken aback, I shot back, "Is there anything left in this world worth laughing about?"

By autumn we couldn't take it anymore. In addition to the hard physical labor and the expensive room and board we were forced to pay with money we no longer had, we were sick and tired of sleeping in the old chicken coop, and con-templated leaving. The straw that broke the camel's back came when we learned that the couple withheld a secret message informing us when and where to meet a group of people that was planning to escape across the border to

France. To us it proved these people were not to be trusted. Helped by Joep Huffener, only 19 years old but very active in the underground movement, we stole away at night. Joep lived on the vast, secluded grounds of the Bergen-Bosch sanatorium that was run by his father. We stayed there happily for a few days until a new place could be found for each of us. Philip became secretary to Kees Boeke, the well-known founder of the first Free School called "De Werkplaats" [1] (the Work Place).

Beactrice and Kees Boeke in 1936

Kees Boeke and his wife Beatrice dedicated their lives to helping others, especially during the years of occupation. Before the war Kees had established an aid organization for Jewish refugees from Germany. During the war the couple arranged schooling for children who had been forced to leave De Werkplaats. They were sheltered by the school staff and later accepted to the school under false names. The workers of De Werkplaats were housed in a separate building. Philip was given a large room on the ground floor, and no one knew his true identity.

I found work as a house servant in a villa that was near enough that we were able to see each other regularly.

In this beautiful autumn we went hiking in the Bilthoven forest, collecting mushrooms to supplement our meager rations. Holland suffered a severe shortage, and food was strictly rationed. We enjoyed these times to the fullest. The forest was taking on hues of red, brown and gold. The birds chirped and sang all around us. We cherished every moment we could be together, especially in nature.

Alas, we received sad news about our families. We were under the impression that Philip's parents had found a reliable hiding place, but we learned that they had been betrayed. In order to give their host some privacy to celebrate their 25th wedding anniversary, they had left their hiding place for two days and were caught. After a short detention in a Rotterdam prison they were deported to Auschwitz and murdered a few days later. Such evil tidings heightened our awareness of the precariousness of our own situation.

In this dark time, every piece of good news was like manna from heaven, and so it was when at long last I received a postcard from Vienna in Liesje' handwriting. It had traveled long and far, passing from hand to hand until it finally reached us. From the careful wording I gathered that Liesje had been released from Bergen-Belsen and was on her way to Palestine. The joy that welled up within me cannot be described. My younger sister was safe! She had survived! There was still hope, then, that one day we would meet again, that is, if I managed to get through this dreadful war alive.

While in Bilthoven, Philip joined the Resistance. Being a military officer he became the commander of a small combat unit of eight men. Philip's name and reputation went before him as a highly self-disciplined man whose discretion could be depended upon. Even I did not know the details of his activities in the Resistance.

In the autumn of 1943, the Germans began firing the terrifying F1 and F2 guided missiles from the coast of Holland against England. Not all of them reached their targets and landed in the surrounding areas. The Dutch Resistance planned to destroy the railway tracks in several places along the route on which the missiles from Germany were transported west. In Bilthoven, the Sanatorium grounds provided a safe hiding place for ammunition and fugitives.

The Germans were deathly afraid of catching tuberculosis and never entered the place. From time to time, the Allies dropped weapons and equipment in the forest not far from the Sanatorium.

On the evening of November 7, 1944, Philip, who was in charge of the mission, and Mach Balk, a young member of the unit who was anxious to prove himself worthy to join the group, rode their bicycles to the meeting place under the cover of darkness. Joep Huffener walked through the woods, bringing the explosives with him. At the moment the unit placed explosives on the railway tracks near the village of Groenekan they were surprised by a German patrol. The three managed to hide under the leaves, as they had trained before. But Mach jumped up in fear when the Germans shot in their direction. After being shot in the legs he was immediately arrested. Philip and Joep managed to get away but Joep fell into the freezing canal. Only after several hours it was safe for him to escape. He contracted double pneumonia and never fully recovered from it.

Philip told me little of this sabotage mission. Tense and anxious I waited all evening in his room for him to return. Suddenly he burst in through the door and hurriedly informed me of what had happened. The mission had failed. He had to flee immediately. At that moment, a neighbor came to the door, ready for a chat. Anxiously, we tried her to leave, but it was too late. The house was completely surrounded. Not only Philip and I, but everyone who happened to be in the house at that hour, were taken to the police station in Bilthoven. Kees Boeke and his wife were later arrested in their home. The next day Mach was taken to Gestapo headquarters in Utrecht. Apparently they tortured him there, thus giving away valuable information which led to further arrests.

Mach was executed the following day in the De Bilt fortress in Utrecht. He was nineteen years old.

The interrogations began that same night and went very badly for Philip. Waiting many long hours outside the room I heard the sounds of beatings, shouts, cursing and screams. Sitting there, face covered with both hands, my body reacted with an intense attack of diarrhea. At first a soldier accompanied me to the toilet. Wanting to keep an eye on me I had to leave the door open. By the fourth time no one paid me attention anymore. Debating whether to throw my false identity card into the toilet, I realized that would be a foolish thing to do. When my turn came it was almost morning. Police ushered me into the room and ordered me to sit facing the wall with my back towards the Dutch interrogator. He did not wish to be recognized.

"Your identity card!" he barked. I handed it to him over my shoulder. After what seemed an eternity of silence, the rustle of papers and shuffling of feet, he shouted, "Where did you get this forged card?" A hammer blow could not have struck harder. I was speechless. The game was over. But suddenly I realized the interrogator could not read my face.
My silence infuriated the man. "Come on, then. Out with it!" he roared. "Where did you get it?" Something in his tone told me that he was not entirely sure of himself.

"The same way you got yours!" I shouted back.

"How dare you be so impertinent!" he screamed at the top of his voice.

"If you shout at me, I'll shout too!" I shot back.
He fed a sheet of paper into the typewriter. Forcing confidence and steadiness in my voice, I coolly answered his questions. At the end of the interrogation a guard took me to a cell.

The next day, three soldiers brought me by car to the Utrecht prison. During the ride my thoughts turned to Philip's weapon. Before the Germans burst in his room I quickly shoved it under the cupboard. Desperate thoughts passed through my mind. If only I had that pistol.....

Inside the Wolvenplein prison

At the Wolvenplein prison, I had to climb many stairs and walk through endless corridors before reaching my cell in the women's section. They put me in solitary confinement. Thank God I was alone. At that moment, I could not have borne the presence of others. Convinced they had nothing to do with the sabotage mission, the staff of "The Vrije School" among them Kees and Beatrice Boeke, were released after a few days. They were not aware of Philip's Jewish identity or of his underground activities. Philip had worked in the offices of the school to reorganize their finances and administration.

It was cold in November. Shivering and overcome with exhaustion after almost two sleepless days and nights I fell asleep. The deep ringing of the bells of the Dom, Utrecht's cathedral, startled me awake.

"You are in a prison cell," I muttered to myself. "The bells are ringing ten o'clock. There is still a long night ahead." Fortune smiled upon me in prison. Because the German female commander was on sick leave my Dutch guard[1] did what she could to make life a bit more comfortable.

The only reading material permitted was the Bible and a prayer book. I asked for the Protestant prayer book, and these two books succored me throughout the long, difficult hours. The Psalms of David in particular gave me strength and solace. While reading the prayers I began to understand that Christianity was not just a religion of the Inquisition and the persecution of the Jews, but that there was another side to it: to spread love throughout the world.

The notorious "Hunger Winter", the Dutch famine of 1944, was just beginning. Sugar beets and flower bulbs were almost all we had to eat. But the food in the Utrecht prison was better than what was available in the villages in the west of Holland. The Swedish Red Cross packages we received contained delicacies we had almost forgotten existed: a piece of cheese, a small block of butter and white bread. In my state of anxiety I felt unable to put anything in my mouth, but the female guard urged me: "Eat, eat now, you will need your strength later."

Thanks to this guard I was able to keep in contact with Philip. He was imprisoned on the same floor, in the men's section.

---

1   An article in the Dutch paper *Het Parool* from 24-12-1945 read, "Guardian Angel. Several political prisoners were saved, thanks to a guard who put her life on the line by helping them. Not only by giving them extra food, but by smuggling notes and giving them important information. She always carried pencil stubs with her so that an important note from a prisoner quickly could be smuggled outside. After the war, Ms. G. Hofstra was honored during a reunion of political prisoners."

If I had been in a cell with other women, this would not have been possible. Just how dangerous contact with other prisoners could be was brought home to me during our daily walk in the inner courtyard. We were led in a long line and forbidden to talk with each other.

That day new prisoners had been brought in - Jewish women who had just been captured. Suddenly I heard a voice behind me: "Aren't you Betty Polak?"

I froze in fear. Not daring to say a word, I quickly shook my head in denial. I was ashamed of my behavior. Perhaps this woman only wanted to ask me for help or advice? But what else could I have done? Once my family name became known I wouldn't stand a chance. Phillips careful answers about how long we had known each other had been reported to me by the guard. Although we had been married for almost five years, he told his interrogators that we knew each other for less than a year. This information saved my life.

I was brought to a magnificent house on the imposing Maliebaan (Boulevard) in Utrecht.

The *Sicherheits Dienst* (SD) had made number 74 their headquarters. What a bitter twist of fate. This house had belonged to the parents of Jewish acquaintances.

Prisoners waiting for their turn to be interrogated were held in big cellars. In there, many were also tortured by the feared SD.

Maliebaan no. 74 in Utrecht.
The boulevard was nicknamed
"Unter den Linden".

For the first five days after our arrest, early in the morning Philip was taken there from his cell and returned late at night. During these days he received neither food nor drink.

I myself was obliged to wait in a cellar for only a few hours. When I was finally led before the German commander[1], his first question was, "How long have you known that Jew?"

Feigning surprise, I said, "Jew? I don't know any Jews."

But he didn't give up. "There is one you most certainly do know. Philip de Leeuw."

That was Philip's real name! I told him I knew someone called Philip, but his family name was van Andel, not De Leeuw.

Sitting in this stately room overlooking the tree lined boulevard, the commander's face was impassive. What should I tell him? Even under torture, Philip had insisted that we had known each other for less than a year. Putting my answer off as long as possible I pretended to consider whether it was ten, or twelve, or perhaps eleven months.

That seemed to convince the commander. He then erupted into a flow of curses. "The evil Jews, the disgusting Jews, the despicable Jews! They destroy the whole world. All the tragedies in the world are their fault!" He made me swear never to have anything to do with that scum, that despicable race.

He continued to ask me strange questions, "Were your parents legally married?"

I smiled, despite the tension I was under. My strictly religious, moral parents would never have imagined anyone accusing them of having a child out of wedlock.

"What are you grinning about? Things like that do happen." He was annoyed. Who knows, perhaps I had touched a nerve?

---

[1] Recent information has brought to light the horrifying deeds of this cruel Oberst Kretär/Head Sipol SD Hermann Neumeier, who was under direct order from Lages. I was the only prisoner who had not been tortured and released. Many prisoners were executed. After the war, he was tried and released after 4 years in prison.

"Show me your hands," he said suddenly and carefully examined each of my fingers.

I had taken off my wedding ring when Philip and I had first gone into hiding. Other rings had been sold to pay for our expenses. Perhaps he was checking to see if there was a mark left by a wedding ring. I looked steadily at him; he then nodded his head towards the door, indicating that I could leave.

Exhausted, I was returned to my cell. The moment I was back within the four walls, I fell to pieces. My bravado deserted me and I felt suffocated by the loneliness. For hours I pounded on the iron door, crying, shouting, "Let me out, let me out of here!", but no one came. In the end I understood that there was nothing left but to accept the reality of my imprisonment and to submit to the inevitable.

A few days later, one of the guards came in to my cell and informed me with some excitement that I was soon to be released. To this day I am still puzzled how quickly this bit of news spread within the prison walls. During my last exercise in the courtyard a guard passed me notes from other prisoners. I hid them in my shoes and my clothes.

The guard brought me a carefully written farewell note from Philip, scribbled in pencil on a scrap of paper. One sentence is forever burnt in my memory: "You always have been the best comrade at my side." This was more precious to me than gold. We both knew his days were numbered.

My belongings were all returned to me. Together with my forged identity card I received my release papers bearing a German stamp. This paper was handed to me personally by the commander with the admonition, "Make sure never to get involved again with anything illegal, and don't ever have anything to do with those who are!"

I thought to myself, if you only knew just how very illegal I am! I turned to leave the room, but he held out his hand and gently said, "You still have time to hand me the notes they gave you. Give them to me now, and nothing will happen to you." I wanted to sink through the floor, but found the strength to answer him coolly, almost smiling, "Do you really think I'm so stupid that I would risk my freedom just to smuggle out some silly notes from prisoners I don't even know?"

And then I was outside, bereft and forlorn. I just wanted to go back to my cell. I didn't want to be free; I didn't know what to do with freedom when Philip was left behind. I had lost all my contacts. In the cold November air I leaned against the large prison gate, unable to take one step.

Betty's release form from prison dated November 17, 1944

An older German soldier standing guard walked up to me. He recognized me from my interrogation trips. "Have they released you?" he asked, and when I hesitantly nodded, he said from the depths of his heart, "How nice for you."

At that moment I couldn't help myself. "What do you know?" I cried. "My life has been ruined. Nothing matters anymore!"

But the sympathetic German did his best to encourage me: "The war will come to an end. You are young; your entire life still lies before you. And now, get away from this place as fast as you can."

That entire day I wandered aimlessly around Utrecht in the forbidding cold, until at last I found myself in a distant neighborhood in a small, cheap inn. There I spent one of the worst nights of my life.

The next morning I returned to Bilthoven, to the home where I worked as a house maid. They received me warmly, but it was awful to find myself shunned by the members of the Resistance. They were sure I had betrayed them, otherwise, how could I have been released? No one believed that a number of fortuitous circumstances, Philip's steadfastness under torture, and a lot of luck combined with my own deceit and impudence had convinced the Germans of my innocence. Much later I had to admit that my behavior at the time could well have been misunderstood. I suffered greatly from their attitude towards me. Without them I could not learn anything about Philip and Pieter ter Beek, another member of Philip's unit who was in the same prison. I had to find my own way. I knew Philip's glasses had been shattered during the violent interrogation, and so I returned to Utrecht with his reserve pair.

When I arrived at the prison, the gate was opened by a familiar Dutch guard. I asked him to give the glasses to Philip. He looked sad when he informed me that he couldn't do that because Philip and two others had been transferred elsewhere. He only knew that Pieter ter Beek was one of them. Pieter was arrested when he went to visit Mach's parents.

"Where are they?" I begged, but the guard couldn't say. "Who does know?" I asked, desperate for any bit of information. "The SD on the Maliebaan," he told me.

"All right then, that's where I'll go." I was determined.

"No! You can't go there!" he cried out in horror. "It is far too dangerous. You're free now! Do you want to be thrown back into prison?"

But where was Philip? What were they doing to him? Unable to live with the uncertainty, I no longer cared if anything happened to me. I was deeply despondent, alone and bereft in the world without my husband, without my family.
Liesje was far away. My parents, my husband's parents, my sister and her husband, my brother and his wife and all my friends were gone. I didn't know if I would ever see any of them again.
So I returned to the dreaded Maliebaan 74, to the *Sicherheitsdienst,* and asked them to take Philip's glasses to him.
They sent me here and there, from one office to the other, until at last I found myself standing before the same Nazi who had interrogated me, in the very same room. He was quite solicitous and even invited me to sit down. On and on he droned about a German soldier who had been shot in Rhenen. The wounded soldier had been able to give detailed information about the people involved. It wasn't clear how many Dutch people had been shot in retaliation for this attack.

But I understood one thing: Philip's fate was sealed. He would be executed by firing squad. But where, and when? And then it hit me. Philip had already been executed.

I forced myself to stay calm. The Nazi took some things from a cupboard and held them out to me – Philip's wristwatch and wedding ring.

"Would you like to have these?" he asked.

"Not interested." Looking him straight in the eyes I stood up and left.

This visit not only proved fruitless, it even heightened the general suspicion under which I was regarded by the Resistance. No Jewish woman would willingly go to the SD headquarters. Who would dare walk into the lion's den just for information, knowing that such behavior could arouse suspicion and put her life in danger? It made me look more suspicious, and in any event put the lives of others at risk, they argued. In my complete self-absorption such a thought had not occurred to me.

But the lives of others were at stake too, it wasn't just about Philip. Even after the war, the insinuations stuck to me. Suspicion lay so deep that I was interrogated for two entire days by the commission that sought to expose and punish those who had betrayed their country. I could not talk about this with anyone, certainly not with my inner circle of friends, each of whom was dealing with their own losses.

Despite having many good friends in Bilthoven, I turned my back on the place. My acquaintances in the Resistance had cut off any contact, and I too disconnected. Their names were erased from my memory. Thus began the long period of silence in my life.

Many years later, my friendship with the Huffener[1] family was restored. After the war Joep married Lotty, a Jewish woman who survived Auschwitz. They had four children. Alas, Joep died at a young age from pneumonia.

Lotty visiting Betty in her home in Holland, 2014

---

[1] Because they risked their own lives to save persecuted Jews, Yad Vashem honored a brother of Joep Huffener, who also risked his life to save Jews, as "Righteous Among the Nations". Joep will be remembered as a fighter against the Germans, but above all of having saved and helped many Jews, like Philip and Betty and the woman he married after the war—Lotty.
Until today, they continue to fight against discrimination and for a better world. Lotty regularly visits schools to share about her life.

Liesje

Atlit 1944

Another warm and sunny day.

I should have been happy, but this morning in Atlit I awoke feeling terribly empty. Slowly I enjoyed my morning ritual. Such a delight: hot running water, real soap, a toothbrush and a new, clean hand towel. Why not savor every moment? I only had myself to look after. But the peace was illusory for I was all on my own. What was I going to do with my life?

Over the next few days I knew a decision had to be made. Those first few days after the long journey from Bergen-Belsen I felt euphoric at having to stay in Atlit. Despite everything I had lost I was grateful to be alive and start anew.

But how? Soon, my sense of overwhelming joy was overtaken by uncertainty, loneliness, depression and even − believe it or not - self pity.

In the dining hall I wasn't able to eat much breakfast. Having been deprived of food for so long, everything I now ate gave me a stomach ache.

"Good morning" I greeted everyone.

Atlit Detention Camp

Today there was no light chatter, no signs of joy.
Everyone seemed troubled by their own thoughts and worries: what next? Where does one go from here?

At the clinic I visited a few friends whose health was being restored thanks to the dedicated care. Outside the barracks the youngest child of our group was playing – three year-old Peter. Early in the war his father had been deported to a death camp. Like a lion, Peter's mother fought to keep him alive. We all adored the little boy. In Atlit he got the first toy in his life: a whistle. First he studied it from all sides, then put it in his mouth and blew. He produced a sound which he knew very well from Bergen-Belsen. Blowing loudly on his whistle, to everyone's horror he yelled, "*Appell! Appell*! (Roll call!)"

The gate entrance pulled me like a magnet. While sitting on a rock I took in my surroundings. Carefully guarded from both sides, no one was allowed to enter or to leave the camp without undergoing a thorough examination. Two towers stood on either end of the camp. However, the guards posted here waved and smiled back at me.

I have been here five days now and it seems I am to be released on Friday morning.
Every day a small group leaves after a medical examination; there is no reason to hold us.
The only question left is: where are we to go?
Family members of those being released gathered on the other side of the fence. I already said goodbye to a family that was allowed to leave: the family Levie. Father, mother and their two daughters were among the lucky ones included in the exchange. In Holland, Miriam had been engaged to Menachem, who had come to Palestine at the beginning of 1938.

(Menachem Bolle was the brother of Freddy, Juul 's husband.)
I watched the scene unfold before me: the family approached
the gate. A final check of their papers, and they were out.
After a separation of six long years, Menachem and Miriam
fell into each other's arms. Embracing tightly, they clung to
each other. Sitting on my rock, I wept.

British bus to transport the detainees

NETHERLANDS—Partially Liberated

BETTY

The south part of the Netherlands was liberated about half a year before the rest of the country, which left almost three quarters still occupied. The standard of living was minimal. There was no fuel, no food supplies, no electricity or telephones. The transportation system – trams and trains – was inoperative and famine reigned all over.

This is how we entered the difficult winter, the famine of 1944-1945, when many people died of starvation.

My sister in law, Suus de Leeuw, found me a hiding place with a friend in Oegstgeest, a small city in the west of Holland not far from Leiden. Piet, as she was called, was divorced with three children. During that time she worked as a social worker in an important factory in Leiden that produced woolen blankets. She invited me to come and live with her and try to

Permit stating she needs her bicycle for Social work and the Wehrmacht is not allowed to confiscate it.

DER REICHSKOMMISSAR
FÜR DIE BESETZTEN NIEDERLÄNDISCHEN GEBIETE
DER REICHSKOMMISSAR
für die besetzten Niederländischen Gebiete
DER BEAUFTRAGTE
für die Provinz Südholland

Leiden, den 23. Dezember 1944

Bescheinigung

Fraeulein Ada K o o l e aus Oegstgeest braucht ihr Fahrrad als soziale Fuersorgerin bei der Firma Gebrs. van ijk & Co. in Leiden und Umgebung zur Ausuebung ihrer sozialen Taetigkeit.

Die Wehrmacht soll gemaess Befehl des W.B.N. das Fahrrad nicht beschlagnahmen.

Diese Bescheinigung gilt nur bis 23. Januar 1945.

I.V.

Verlaengert bis 23.Februar 1945

recuperate. Piet often rode to the country on her bicycle with its wooden wheels to barter wool with the farmers in exchange for food. But after a while even the farmers in this part of the country had nothing left to exchange.

In the eastern part of the country, near the German border, the farmers still had plenty. Since I had a lot of free time, I took it upon myself to exchange the wonderful wool for food for our 'family'. After all, Piet was working hard and had to take care of her children. Because of her work she obtained an official bicycle permit. This was of great value since the Germans had confiscated all bicycles, old and new, and continued to do so at every checkpoint.

One day, Piet's mother fell ill and needed help. She lived in the Eastern part of Holland, on the other side of the IJssel river, about a day's journey from Oegstgeest. This closed region could not be entered without an authorization. With my false identity card I obtained a permit at the German police station. I felt safe enough to visit Piet's mother several times.

Special travel permit

119

Picture of the Hunger Winter: women carrying food on tireless - or bicycles with wooden tires.

From there I cycled to the rural area near the border with Germany. The farmers were delighted with the beautiful wool and in return took good care of me; I was invited to join them at their table for nutritious meals and always had a place to sleep. Returning to Oegstgeest loaded with bread, eggs, sausages, butter, ham, potatoes and other goodies – all the staple foods so vital that winter, their joy knew no bounds. Thanks to my fluent German, none of my goodies were ever confiscated at one of the many roadblocks. That was quite exceptional.

In this eastern zone, I always stayed a few days in Balkbrug with the family of the school director. On Sundays I accompanied them to church, just like one of the family. The peaceful and serene atmosphere soothed my soul and gave meaning to my life.

My food expeditions were becoming increasingly risky.

We found ourselves caught between a rock and a hard place: on the one hand there were the feared German V1 and V2 missiles; on the other hand we often had to hide when the Allied warplanes began shelling and shooting at anything that moved. One day I caught a ride with a big truck; they unloaded me in Utrecht with my bicycle, laden down with food. It was already eight o'clock in the evening, past curfew. No one was allowed on the streets at such an hour, but I had no choice. Utrecht and its formidable prison held terrible memories for me. I hated the city and tried to get out as fast as I could. The noise of my wooden wheels probably alerted two German soldiers.

"What are you doing at this hour?" they shouted and stopped me.

"I'm bringing food to my starving family in West Holland," I yelled back. "I have to go on. If you plan to arrest me, you'll better shoot me on the spot."
After conferring with one another they ordered, "Wait here and don't move!" Upon their return each rode a bicycle and a big rifle slung across their shoulder. Gallantly they told me,

"It is far too dangerous for a young lady to ride alone at night through the city. We have been instructed to accompany you to the edge of town where it will be safer for you to continue on your way."
That was the safest trip I had in my whole life! Greatly relieved I continued my journey, although after the German soldiers left me, I had to ride all alone in the pitch darkness.

The famine in the west was horrific. We cooked our food on smoldering woodchips. When these ran out, we decided to take apart the garden gate, only to discover early the next morning that others had been there before us - the gate was gone. There was no choice but to burn the chairs and other pieces of furniture. People were collapsing and dying of hunger in the streets. Awful sights became a daily reality.
The gradual liberation of Europe from the Nazi occupation was scarcely noticeable. Everything centered on the struggle

to survive, that is, the search for food. All we talked about was food. Cooking over tiny flames fed by straw and stubble took up the better part of the day. Our 'family's' situation was good compared to most, thanks to my excursions to the eastern part of the Netherlands.

Just a month before all of Holland was liberated, I stopped at a small coffee shop to get something to drink. The radio broadcast announced that the President of the USA, Theodor Roosevelt, had died on the 12th of April. With a shock it dawned on me that another world existed beyond my own country, where people were mostly pre-occupied with the question of when this war would end at long last!
In the meantime the wool, our sole bartering commodity, had run out. There was no point in continuing any Hunger Expeditions. To relieve Piet of the responsibility of one more mouth to feed, I decided to travel to the Nabarro family in Amersfoort, whom I knew well. Paying a small fortune to acquire Aryan certificates, the Nabarro family had been able to remain in their spacious home. They kindly sheltered me until the end of the war.

Fragments of Letters from Betty to Liesje

May 3, 1945

My darling little sister,
From the day you left Holland my thoughts have been with you continually. How I have longed to run to you, to embrace you, to talk with you. It has been almost three years since we last saw each other and it may take another year before I am able to come to you.
And if we do manage to meet again, what will it be like?
Have you changed as much as I have, in these war years?

Will we still be as close as we once were? I do hope so. Yes, I am sure of it, because I felt so close to you throughout the entire war.

We have led very different lives, Liesje, and I think that will be true in the future also. My life has completely changed. You will probably be astounded by my views on life and people, and the Jewish problem. It's not just because of Flip's death. Even before the war Flip and I changed our plans about making Aliya to Palestine and work there with our hands. And today my opinions are even stronger than before.

I have been through so much. After Flip died I traveled from west to east and back again to gather food for people in the city. Famine was widespread, people were starving. Thanks to the Gestapo stamp on my official release papers from prison, my false identity as Adrie Kool was secure. I kept thinking, if only I could speak with you, to share with you what I was going through.

And now the situation is like this: there are no trains, no buses, no trams or any other transportation, just our feet. To get from place to place I have to ride my bicycle with its wooden wheels! Hunger is everywhere. People are collapsing in the streets, but one can still get a few things from the farmers in the villages. That's why I go out there every day.

Let me hear from you soon. I embrace you, again and again,
Betty

Amersfoort

By the time I reached Amersfoort, the Canadian army was stationed only 40 kilometers east of the city. News reports of battles in Zutphen, Deventer and Apeldoorn were highly alarming. After having been only a few days with the Nabarros I became restless and decided to return to Amsterdam.

The end of the war was already in the air. On the way to the big city I saw the Germans destroying installations and equipment in order to prevent them from falling into the hands of the enemy. They saw fit to destroy absolutely everything!

On Passover Eve I wanted to share the Seder meal with my friends Jeanne and Truus van Amerongen, Lion Nordheim and Bram Pais [1], who lived under false identities in a secret apartment. But to my consternation I found no one there.

Deeply concerned, even though it was already well past curfew, I cycled to the home of the Querido family. Once the psychiatric institution had been emptied of its inhabitants, the couple had been allowed to return to their home in Amsterdam. On my way to them I found hundreds of pamphlets that had been thrown from Allied aircraft. The Querido's were excited to read the Allied Forces' demands: "I SURRENDER!" was written in big German letters.

When I finally found out that the friends I planned to meet had been arrested, there was nothing left to do in Amsterdam. Liberation was just around the corner, but the Germans were still arresting Jews! In one week I had covered over 325 kilometers on my rickety bicycle. But despite my exhaustion I wanted to leave Amsterdam. The journey back to Amersfoort was surreal. The rattle of my wooden wheels added to the noise of the Allied aircraft's continued air attacks. Riding through expansive woods I passed troops of German soldiers camping with their horses, buggies, cows and anything else imaginable.

---

[1] My friends lived under false identities in their secret apartment. Leon, one of the leaders of the Youth Zionist Movement before the war, a unique man of vision with strongly Semitic features, was shot. Jeanne and Truus van Amerongen survived and moved to Israel after the war. Thanks to the courageous intervention of a non-Jewish girlfriend Bram Pais survived After the war he became a famous physicist and collaborated with Robert Oppenheimer and Albert Einstein in the USA nuclear research program.

SCHLUSSMACHEN
bedeutet:

FÜR DEUTSCHLAND -

Einen harten aber gerechten Frieden, in dem man leben können wird.

Präsident Roosevelt erklärte in seinem Bericht über die Beschlüsse der Dreimächtekonferenz in Yalta : „Bedingungslose Kapitulation bedeutet nicht die Vernichtung oder Versklavung des deutschen Volkes... Wir werden nicht wieder, wie nach dem vorigen Krieg, in den Fehler verfallen, Wiedergutmachung in Geldleistungen zu verlangen, die Deutschland niemals aufbringen kann. Wir wollen nicht, dass das deutsche Volk Hunger leidet oder eine Last für die übrige Welt wird."

FÜR DICH -

Den Schutz der Genfer Konvention. Allein im Westen haben sich bisher über 1 000 000 deutsche Soldaten unter diesen Schutz gestellt, indem sie sich in hoffnungsloser Lage ergaben. Als Kriegsgefangenem stehen Dir die folgenden Vergünstigungen zu:

1. Sofortige Entfernung aus der Kampfzone
2. Verpflegung wie die der alliierten Truppen
3. Dieselbe Lazarettpflege wie die der Alliierten
4. Regelmässiger Postverkehr mit der Heimat
5. Baldmöglichste Heimkehr nach Kriegsende

Wenn Du Schluss machen musst, so lege Waffen, Helm und Koppel ab. Hebe die Hände, schwenke etwas Weisses, und rufe den alliierten Soldaten zu: **EI SURRENDER !**

Sample of the many pamphlets that the Allies dropped over Nazi occupied territories. At the bottom of the pamphlet it says: "I surrender" in German phonetics.

Riding as slowly as possible I tried to take in the bizarre scenes: half naked men were washing themselves by a table made of tree stubs; an officer was sitting alone in the middle of the woods, completely sunken in thought, playing an organ. A bit further, a group of soldiers were singing while polishing their boots. Were they getting ready for the final battle?

"The Germans have no lack of food," I thought a moment before I almost crashed into a soldier running across the road holding large containers of butter.

Reaching Amersfoort on the 18th of April, the city was quiet and still. The next day everything changed. We were directly in the line of fire.

The last weeks in Amersfoort were very tense. From the Nabarro house on the main street we watched the movements of the German troops and high-ranking officers. Generals rode back and forth to secret discussions in Wageningen, near Arnhem. The battles were constant and the sounds of explosions never stopped. Even "Long Jan", the magnificent tower of the ancient cathedral, became a target. The inhabitants of Amersfoort raged against the Germans when the pride of their city went up in flames. Everyone prayed with all their hearts that the battles would end. But they continued much longer than anyone had expected. In other regions in Holland the Allied Forced were re-conquering tens of kilometers each day, but near Amersfoort – or so it seemed to us – they only crept forward meter by meter. Constantly we had to run down to the bomb shelter. We almost lived there. Worst of all was the shortage of water. The only place to get water (once a day) was from the city pump in the center of town. For hours on end we stood in line for the pump, and were hard pressed to get back home in time for the six o'clock curfew. One evening, when at last our turn came, a German policeman jumped the queue, a buggy attached to a horse. We had to wait for him to leave, but were utterly pleased to see that the Germans had their difficulties too. As we trudged home, our arms weighed down with buckets of water for another day, we knew for certain: the end of the Second World War was drawing near. Despite the danger, whenever we could we ran to the sidewalk to follow the action. A never-ending stream of German soldiers marched by, laden with equipment, exhausted, leaning on each other. Nothing in them evoked the memory of the proud lords of the New World Order. Like thieves in the night the soldiers of the third Reich slipped out of Holland, humiliated, their spirits broken.

Feeling neither hatred nor joy the eternal question would not leave me alone: the world could be so harmonious and balanced. Why, oh why, must the good suffer so much from the evil in this life?

A few days later, an eerie silence fell upon our area. No longer did we hear shelling. The quiet was unreal, almost scary. Eight cars full of high ranking German officers sped towards Hoevelaken for peace talks with the British victors. The announcement was made later: a twenty-four hour truce had been declared! The previous desolate and deserted streets suddenly filled with crowds of people.

The joy was overwhelming.

Low flying big planes dropped food parcels to the starving population. Tons of goods. No more bombs. The war was over.

American plane dropping food

Allied troops entering Amersfoort

Headline: *War in Europe has ended. May 5, 1945*

Amersfoort celebrates

PHILIP

Betty's Letter to Liesje

May 5, 1945

Dear Sister,
The first day of peace began with mixed feelings. Philip, who so yearned for this moment, did not live to see it. I have to go on without him. And now? Who has survived, and who has not? I am so afraid of what lies ahead. Only one thing gives me courage and strength: I can write to you once more, even if it takes forever for you to receive my letters.
My dear, sweet sister, tell me everything. Do not let the strong cords that bound us throughout the war be lost now, even if I am not the same girl you knew before.

Betty

The sun was shining. People were lined up along the streets, cheering the Canadians as their tanks rolled into Amersfoort. It was an exhilarating sight, but I could not share in everyone's joy. Hardly a syllable came out of my mouth. Philip had so longed for this moment; we had talked often of the victory we both yearned for. Our marriage lasted almost five years, but we had been forced to live separately most of the time. His death at the age of thirty left a huge void in my life.

Amersfoort cheered and celebrated. I couldn't.

First I had to find out what exactly happened to Philip.

The police informed me that in the afternoon of November 20, 1944, six young men, one of them Philip, had been shot by a firing squad in the woods of Prattenberg on the border between Rhenen and Veenendaal. The youngest of them was still a minor.

Among them was also the Protestant Reverend Bastiaan Jan Ader. He had seen it as his holy duty to save Jews and many others. A collaborating Dutch policeman, whom he trusted, betrayed him. On the long day before the execution he continuously comforted his fellow prisoners and sustained them with texts from the Bible. It was almost dark when the men were ordered to line up in front of the firing squad. Reverend Ader asked the German commander if he was allowed to pray the "Our Father" with his companions, which was granted.[1] The Germans issued an edict that the bodies were to be left in the forest for 24 hours to serve as a deterrent to others.

The Lord's Prayer

Our Father, who art in heaven,
Hallowed be Thy Name.
Thy kingdom come.
Thy will be done,
On earth as it is in heaven.
Give us this day our daily bread.
And forgive us our trespasses,
As we forgive those
who trespass against us.
And lead us not into temptation,
But deliver us from evil.
For Thine is the kingdom
And the power, and the glory,
For ever and ever.
Amen.

[1] Recently, more information about this dark chapter in history has emerged, adding more pieces to the puzzle. A history teacher at the Ichtus College in Veenendaal is actively researching the event and people that were involved. See blog for updated information.

So they lay there, until the inhabitants of Veenendaal were permitted to bury them in a make-shift grave in their city cemetery.

Following their execution the Royal Netherlands Marechaussee[1] took pictures of the bodies which were sent to the families of the victims. Only after the war I received the terrible picture which I kept in my wallet with his farewell note. But even these two last mementos were denied me: my wallet was stolen.

Post-war times were chaotic. The bodies of the executed men had to be moved from their temporary graves as soon as possible. Not properly registered anywhere, Philip was the only one of the six who had not found a permanent resting place. The police informed me that I had to arrange for his burial very soon. But how? We had lived in so many different places that no longer had any meaning for me.

Suus, my sister-in-law, and I decided to bury him in the cemetery in Veenendaal, the town where Philip and his comrades had been executed.

On a warm day in May, Suus and I left Amersfoort for Veenendaal, catching rides along the way because public transportation was not yet running. When at long last we arrived at the cemetery, our arms filled with wilted flowers, we were too late for the funeral. The gravedigger tried to console me,

"It's just as well you weren't here, Ma'am," he said. "It stank terribly, which is always the case with second burials."

[1] Royal Netherlands Marechaussee (Royal Military Constabulary) is a Dutch Gendarmerie Force performing military police and civil police duties.

Later, a memorial was erected in the woods where the six men had lost their lives – a white cross, a stone engraved with their names, a short text and a few flower boxes.

The inhabitants of Veenendaal still feel connected to the victims of the German revenge. Twice a year they hold a moving ceremony at the memorial site in the forest, the first on May 4, the Dutch national day of mourning; and the second on November 20, the date Philip and the five others were executed.

A few years later, my husband's remains were laid to rest at the beautiful war cemetery in the Loenen forest. Each grave has a simple headstone surrounded by a lot of space.

Loenen War Cemetery

I didn't arrive in time for the third funeral either. After losing my way in the woods I finally found my husband's fresh grave. The gravediggers explained in apology, "A second burial - and a third

132

in this case - has to be done as quickly as possible."

The 4th of May is the Dutch national Memorial Day for victims of World War II. All over the country, thousands of people visit memorial sites and graves of those who gave their lives for freedom. The Netherlands War Graves Foundation tends these graves in keeping with its motto: "That They May Rest in Honor".

I will never forget Bastiaan Ader. Each time I visit the Loenen cemetery, I put fresh flowers on his final resting place.

Betty at the 2013 Memorial Service in Veenendaal

THE SEARCH FOR SURVIVORS

After the war, I returned to Amsterdam to get information about family and friends.

Everyone who managed to survive the war was looking for relatives and friends. There were long lists of names, descriptions and information of lost ones. Parents searched for their children who had been hidden all over the country. Women searched for their husbands, men searched for their wives.

Many times I made the rounds to every possible office.

People with a common family name like ours (Polak) had to wait for hours in line. I got more and more depressed. After all my efforts failed, I placed advertisements in the newspapers. But the faces of those who were helping me grew more troubled from day to day.

In June 1945, two months after the war ended, news spread that survivors of the Bergen-Belsen concentration camp had arrived at the Philips Factory in Eindhoven.

Among them were people from the death trains who had been travelling around Germany for two weeks before being freed by the Red Army near Tröbitz (formerly the DDR) on April 23, 1945. It had taken so long for them to arrive because of the chaos in Europe. The survivors were quarantined in the buildings of the Philips factory.

The two southern provinces of The Netherlands, Limburg and North Brabant, had been liberated in 1944, about half a year before the rest of the country. Even though the southern part of the country was a closed military zone, I decided to try my luck.

My cousin Bep Duizend, who survived the war in hiding, worked in the reopened Jewish hospital in Amsterdam. She lent me one of her uniforms which helped me get through the military checkpoints. Hitching a ride on a big truck, we were stopped by American soldiers, who saw a nurse – me. There had been an accident, and they needed my help.

The only thing I remembered from a first-aid course was: if you don't know what to do, don't do anything at all!

Approaching the injured people, I shook my head and said convincingly, "Call a qualified doctor! To my regret, I cannot help here.

At the enormous Philips factory compound, I evaded the doctors who urgently sought my help.

Finally, I found a group of survivors at the radiology department on the top floor, waiting to be checked.

Thanks to my uniform, nobody stopped me. I looked at the men, one by one. They were just skin and bones!

Suddenly someone called my name. It was so soft that I was not sure I had heard, "Betty. Betty, is it you? Is it really you?"

Only after looking intently did I recognize one of the walking skeletons: it was my brother Jaap (Jack)! Standing next to him was my cousin, Harry Duizend, Bep's brother! We stared at each other, uncomprehending, as if we were from two different worlds. Afraid they would break in my arms, I carefully embraced Jaap (Jack) and my cousin.

"Please go downstairs," Jaap (Jack) said with difficulty. "Manja is there and other women you know. See what you can do for them and try to arrange for us to get back to Amsterdam."

In the women's ward I had another shock. Despite all the reports that had filtered through about the conditions in the camps, I was not prepared for what followed.

The floor of the long hall was covered with mattresses. On them lay women who were just skin and bones. "Lay your pistol down, babe," the happy music of the American Andrew Sisters, forbidden throughout the war, intensified the surrealistic atmosphere.

I couldn't get near enough to the women to assist them or to make them more comfortable. At first I found it hard to make out who was who, including Manja. They were all very concerned for their families and friends, and worried about what would happen next. Suddenly it was clear what I could do to help. At the end of the long day I went back to Amsterdam with lists of names, addresses, letters and messages.

Determined to never use it again I returned the nurse uniform to my cousin.

The search didn't end there. People also sought to have their property restored, their homes and personal possessions.

The money in their bank accounts and their insurances had to be evaluated. In postwar Netherlands this was not easy. The bureaucracy threw all kinds of incomprehensible obstacles in our paths. People were let down by friends and neighbors who had been trusted with their belongings. Alas, the guilt of stealing another's property was not compatible with a fresh start, not to speak of the lack of sympathy and understanding. When Philip and I had gone into hiding, we had entrusted clothes, tools and other possessions to one of the workers at the Apeldoornsche Bosch. Philip, whose hobby was breeding long-eared rabbits, had given the man everything he had acquired for safekeeping. As I had almost nothing left to wear, I traveled to Apeldoorn as soon as I could to fetch my clothes.

While I made my way up to the house I saw the woman in the garden, hanging up her laundry. She was wearing a cute summer dress, one I immediately recognized as my own. Among the pieces on the line I saw many of my own clothes.

I stood there for a while, looking at her before I could bring myself to go up and ask her about my belongings. "No, I'm sorry", she lied brazenly, "I gave everything away. It was too dangerous to keep your things."

Silently, I turned around and walked away. I would never return to Apeldoorn.

My brother had survived. My sister was training to be a nurse in Palestine. Dries, my brother-in-law, who had become a pilot in the Royal Air Force was soon to return to the Netherlands. Why couldn't I be grateful for the fact that three of the four children in our family were alive? I was not able to support those who had returned from the camps.

In order to come to terms with my losses, I needed a profession that would take all my energy. Only after being free of my memories would I be able to help others.

After the war, nobody paid condolences visits.

Everyone, including me, was busy repressing their losses. Unable to express my grief for my husband, my parents, my sister Juul and the many relatives and friends that I lost, Queen Wilhelmina's letter touched me deeply. (See next page.)

She praised Philip's heroism in the Resistance, spoke of her gratitude for his sacrifice and expressed her sympathy.

Only after reading these condolences did I find myself able to truly grieve. I mourned for all the people that had been lost, for my youth, my marriage, for all that had been taken from me, and for a world that no longer existed.

'S GRAVENHAGE, 7 Februari 1947.
HUIS HOUSENHAGE

Mevrouw de Wed. B. de Leeuw-Polak,
Emmastraat 27,
's-G R A V E N H A G E.

Als lid van den Orde Dienst en Commandant
van de plaatselijke K.P. werd Uw echtgenoot
Philip, Reserve 1e Luitenant, op 20 November
1944 te Rhenen op laaghartige wijze van het
leven beroofd.
     Met diepe gevoelens van medeleven kom Ik
U bij dit voor U zoo zware verlies Mijn oprech-
te deelneming betuigen.
     Zijn offer zal door Mij steeds in dankba-
re herinnering gehouden worden.
     Moge zijn nagedachtenis U een steun in
het verdere leven blijven.

Queen Wilhelmina

1947

The Hague, Noordeinde Palace ,
                   February 7,1947

Mrs. Widow B. de Leeuw-Polak,
Emmastraat 27
     's Gravenhage (The Hague)

     As a member of the military and of-
ficer in the K.P., your husband Philip,
First Lieutenant in the Reserve Army, was
robbed of his life on 20 November 1944 in
Rhenen in a despicable way.
     With deepest sympathy I assure you of
my honest condolences for your terrible
loss.
     I will always remember your husband's
sacrifice with gratitude.
     May his memory be a support to you in
your future life.

BRITISH MANDATE PALESTINE

Letters from Liesje to Betty

July 9, 1945

Dear Sister,

Where should I begin? The last letter I wrote you was from Westerbork, before we were taken to Bergen-Belsen. I don't even know if you ever got it. So much has happened since then. It is hard to believe that now I can write to you again. You have survived; so have I. And I can finally write just as I like. Be assured of one thing: I have written many, many letters to you in my thoughts. I read your first letter over and over. It is rather damp now, from the tears I have shed over it. Cousin Joop and his wife Lida received me warmly in their small apartment in Jerusalem. They have a little daughter, Elisheva, three years old.

From her own scanty wardrobe Lida gave me some of her clothes. The first Sabbath evening was very hard for me. I couldn't speak. Everything reminded me so much of home.

Lida and Joop are Orthodox, and Joop said Kiddush over the wine and the bread. They were so tactful. They didn't ask any questions and neither did I, knowing that their parents, just like ours, were sent to Sobibor and most certainly are no longer alive.

Besides, I found it very difficult to pray.

I didn't know what to do with this God. A God who took away our parents, who allowed your Flip to be executed, who let Juul die just ten days after liberation. I just didn't want anything more to do with God and religion.

I want to complete my nursing training as soon as possible, in the best hospital there is, so two days after arriving in Jerusalem I went to Hadassah Hospital on Mount Scopus. I asked to speak with the director, and was brought to her immediately. Mrs. Cantor[1] was an imposing, extraordinarily beautiful woman wearing a starched and ironed uniform, and a white cap on her gray hair. She made an enormous impression on me.
I heard later that all the student nurses are quite in awe of her.
The biggest problem for me was the language. At the time I couldn't speak more than ten Hebrew words. Now, after almost a year, I can't imagine where I found the courage to go to Hadassah. If I had even suspected what difficulties lay ahead, I may never have gone. But perhaps it is better not to know today what tomorrow will bring. I spoke to her in English, telling her I was a nursing student and would like to complete my studies.

[1] **Shulamith Cantor** (Frieda Jedid Halevi) had studied at the nursing school of the American University in Beirut and came to Mandate Palestine in 1919 as a stowaway. As a widow with 4 children in 1934 she directed the Hadassah School of Nursing in Jerusalem (later the Henrietta Szold Hadassah-Hebrew University School of Nursing), and was a leader and founder of the nursing profession in Palestine during the British Mandate Period (1920–1948) and the first years of statehood. She had a clear conception of nursing as a profession and worked determinedly towards its adoption in the society taking shape in Palestine. Shulamith Cantor died in December 1979.

She was very kind. The admissions committee consisted of seven "VIP's" sitting around the table. They included Dr. Chaim Yassky, the Director of the hospital, Mrs. Cantor, Director of the nursing school and Mrs. Landsman from Hadassah in the U.S. Looking at those important people, I thought, "How nice! They are all Jewish; I don't have to be afraid."

The first thing they asked was, "How do you expect to study when you do not speak the language?" I answered in my best Hebrew, "I have a month. I will spend it on a kibbutz. And I will learn to speak Hebrew." They all laughed and said, "That's something we'd like to see!" Fortunately, I was accepted, but had to start all over again because they couldn't place me in the second year. What was there to lose? I needed a roof over my head, a bed, food and hot water, at least until this damned war was over. And then I would see.

My friend Channa lives in Kibbutz Yavne. She was lucky enough to come to Palestine on the last youth transport before the war broke out. I was invited to come and stay with her for a month. Channa's parents and little brother had not been in Westerbork, and I never met them. Unable to tell her anything, I consoled her with the thought that perhaps they had gone into hiding or managed to flee.[1]

I had a wonderful time in Yavne. Not that I learned much Hebrew there, but I did find some peace. Do you know what a kibbutz is? Young people form a community, and everyone works as hard as he or she is able. The profits are shared by everyone. The larger the profits, the more they are able to expand and develop. The kibbutz began with tents and wooden shacks, the stone buildings came later. Of course, the married couples were the first to move in to these.

---

[1] After the war we learned that they had attempted to enter Switzerland only to be sent back. They lived in hiding in Belgium and came to Israel after the war. Channa's father was killed in a bomb explosion in Tel Aviv in 1949.

Channna was still single, so I lived with her in a wooden shack. There were quite a few young single men. It wasn't long before one of them began paying me particular attention. We strolled "in the moonlight", and within a week he told me he loved me. "Will you marry me?"

Despite the acne blemishes on his nose he was a nice boy, but I wasn't in love with him.

"First I am going to nursing school for three years in Jerusalem," I told him. "I'm sure that in the meantime you'll find a nice girl. And if you don't, I promise to give the matter more thought." That was the end of his love for me.

The next candidate volunteered to teach me Hebrew (and other things I was not interested in). He too wanted to marry me, so I gave him the same answer. We parted as friends.

The third (Dutch) suitor drove me mad by constantly speaking about the war. After a week he earnestly suggested we get married. I wished him all the best, but not with me!

Confronting Channa, I demanded, "What is going on here? Why are all the boys running after me?"

My friend finally let the cat out of the bag, "We're very short on girls on the kibbutz, and in our last meeting we decided that every girl who comes to visit must be persuaded to stay. The unmarried boys were told, "Get married as quickly as you can - love will follow later!" "

July 12, 1945

I've been writing to you a lot lately, as if to catch up on everything we have missed. So... that day in Hadassah in September, 1944. For the first time ever I was in an exclusively Hebrew-speaking environment. Most of the 35 student nurses were about 18 years old. Being the oldest among them, almost 23, I simply followed them around. When they called in my direction I said "ken", which means "yes" in Hebrew.

Having been accepted to the program rather late, there was no place for me in the first-year dormitory. I shared a room with second year students, some of whom knew German, which was a great help.

Liesje →

During classes I couldn't understand a word of what the teacher was saying. By the time I found the word in the Dutch-Hebrew dictionary, the lesson was almost over. Neither could I understand the patients in the ward. Most of the girls are Sabras, a nickname for those born here. A sabra is a cactus fruit, a "prickly pear", prickly on the outside, but soft and deliciously sweet on the inside. I am the first Dutch girl to study at Hadassah Hospital. My fellow students are nice and willing to help, but they don't have much patience.

I am still amazed that I somehow managed to get through the first year. My Hebrew is pretty good now. Luckily we were taught many languages and the Yiddish I lack, I learn from the patients.

The population here can be divided into three groups: Sabras, who were born here, 'Yekim'[1] who fled Germany before the war, and those from Eastern Europe.

---

[1] They were called 'Yekim' (Yekke) because they always wore a jacket ("Jacke" in German), even on a hot day, and took great care to dress well under any circumstance.

The Sabras are young, strong, very cheerful, athletic, nice and kind-hearted. The Yekim are the exact opposite: they remind me of the bourgeoisie in Amsterdam. The East European Jews are mostly poor but they have good hearts. I don't understand their customs well, but enjoy taking care of them because they are sensitive and appreciative. The Yemenites speak a special kind of Hebrew, are very clean and meticulous, religious, intelligent, and they have beautiful faces and gorgeous eyes. I really love them!

Those of us who had not yet learned Hebrew had to pass a special exam. We had to read three books in Hebrew, ten poems by Chaim Nachman Bialik, study the Bible, and learn grammar and so on. I loved Bialik's poems because you gave Father a special edition of his poems for his birthday, one of the last we celebrated. As we were required to recite one poem from memory, I chose the shortest and cutest – the children's blessing for the food. (See next page)

"How long did Methuselah live and when?" they asked during the Bible exam. I had no idea who he was. Luckily they decided to let all the girls pass.

July 16, 1945

It's very difficult to get to the city on Shabbat. The hospital is on Mt. Scopus, about an hour's walk from the center. We are forbidden to use the Arab buses, and it is too dangerous to walk alone. The only possible way to get to the city on Shabbat is by Jewish taxi.

ברכת הַמָּזוֹן   *Birkat haMazon*

Blessed be the Lord	בָּרוּךְ הָאֵל	Baruch haEl
Who created	אֲשֶׁר בָּרָא	Asher bara
A bowl full	דַּיְסָה בְּחָלָב	Daysa bechalav
Of milky porridge	מְלֹא הַקְּעָרָה,	Melo hake'arah
And for dessert	וּלְקִנּוּחַ	Oelekinooach
An apple	גַּם תַּפּוּחַ.	Gam tapoeach
How can we thank Him?	בַּמֶּה, בַּמֶּה נוֹדֶה לוֹ?	Bameh, bameh node lo?
Blessed be He,	בָּרוּךְ הוּא	Baroech hu
Blessed be His Name.	וּבָרוּךְ שְׁמוֹ!	Oevaruch Shemo.

Mt. Scopus (Har Hatsofim) Nursing School and student nurses

Most of the patients suffer from malaria or hepatitis, and there are a few cases of typhus. That doesn't prevent them from using their eyes. They are, on the whole, nice boys who are acquainted with all the nurses and know when the new shift begins. There is an annoying custom in the hospital: student nurses have to wear a shorter cap until the end of their trial period. It makes them very conspicuous. The other students have a regular cap.

Our shift begins at 2 o'clock in the afternoon with a ritual called "preparing for the night". I was sent to the men's ward. Most of the young fellows are delighted to have pretty young girls looking after them. They tease them, and my friends know how to put them in their place. But me? I could hardly understand what they were saying, let alone answer back. That suited them just fine.

"Nurse, bring me a cup of tea"; "Nurse, I don't feel well, put your hand on my forehead, I think I have a fever"; and "Nurse, Nurse, quickly! The bedpan!"

Instead of telling them to go to hell, I scurried back and forth and eventually fled the ward in tears. The next day I went to Mrs. Cantor and asked her to place me in a small, quiet ward with only women, at least until I spoke better Hebrew. She understood, and I was transferred to the gynecological ward, where I felt a lot better.

Betty, I have something to confess. I am afraid the water bill at the hospital must have gone through the roof. From Westerbork I wrote that my happiest moments were spent in my weekly shower. In Bergen-Belsen the situation was much worse.

And now, imagine, I have a shower all to myself and all the water I could wish for. I stand there for hours, terribly afraid the other girls will find me out. It would be so embarrassing.

I enjoy the privacy of the toilets all the more, where no one can see me.

In the war we lacked even the most essential items. Here in the hospital, next to each wash basin is a bar of soap. The first time I noticed that, I quickly slipped it into my pocket. In case there wouldn't be any more. The following days I continued to take a piece of soap and hid it in the back of my cupboard. It gave me such a nice feeling: "Come what may, at least I have enough soap!"

This went on for quite some time until I noticed that I really didn't need such a stack of soap. I put it all back. Luckily my strange collection was not discovered, lest they would have thought me a thief!

July 29, 1945

School will be closed in August and all the girls are going 'home'. Having no home, I have to find somewhere to stay for four weeks. My financial situation is dismal. Certainly the girls here noticed why I never joined them for a cup of coffee. I don't want them to pay for me. Sometimes I long to buy a bar of chocolate, but that is impossible.

For a while I tried to earn money on the side, knitting for a handcraft shop, but I had to give that up rather quickly. It was too tiring to study and work at the same time.

My holidays will be divided up between various friends - a few days here, a few days there, and then in the end I will go to Kibbutz Yavne. I would much rather stay in one place and rest properly, but I can't. On the other hand, how fortunate I am to have friends in so many different places.

August 18, 1945

One day I accompanied the doctor on his rounds. Zechariah was in the last room – a Yemenite with beautiful black eyes and a large gray-black beard. Propped up in the pillows he gazed into the beautiful garden surrounding the hospital.

On a clear day you can see as far as the Dead Sea. The gravely ill man looked much older than his years. It was not the first time he had been in the hospital, but he could never give us specific times and dates.

"Zecharia, think hard", the doctor urged him. "We really must know when you were last admitted to the hospital."

While making an effort to remember, he helplessly looked at the doctor. Then his eyes lit up, and he pointed to the garden.

"Doctor, do you see those trees? The first time, they were just little saplings. The second time you treated me, they had grown this much." He stretched out his arms to indicate their height. "They were four years old. And now I'm in here for the third time, and do you see how big and beautiful the trees are now?"

Zecharia had no idea of dates and years but he was able to explain the passing of time by the trees. After all, he had been the hospital's gardener throughout all those years!

The new Hadassah School of Nursing on Mt. Scopus. Landscaping still in progress.

Letter from Betty to Liesje

August 19, 1945

Dear Sister,
Please keep all my letters about the war and the liberation.
Already now I have difficulty remembering how hard it was.
Even the most awful experiences quickly fade from memory.
Perhaps it is a blessing, how else could we go on with our
lives? We have to look forward, build a new meaningful LIFE,
while making the best of things. Write soon!
*With much love, **Betty***

Letters from Liesje to Betty 1945 -1947

September 1, 1945

Dear Betty,
You asked if I have a boyfriend. There are plenty of nice men
here who would like to start up something, but it is hard to
ascertain what their intentions are. Just sex? To date? To
pass the time? They don't seem serious at all. Some of the
young doctors are quite nice. Being at the beginning of their
careers they look for a girl with wealthy parents so that they
can begin practicing medicine with a good financial base.
Well, they can forget about me then.
Did I tell you that I received a package in the mail at New
Years? It didn't have a return address. When I opened the
pretty box, I found a silver brooch lying on velvet. Two little
grape leaves, so beautiful. The secret sender included a note,
"From a patient who will never forget you."
I was confused and touched. Who could have sent it? I never
found out, but I cherish this gift.

Back to the boys who are running after me. I am older than most of the girls in the nursing school. It makes a difference if you fall in love when you are 17 or 23.

I go out with all kinds of friends. On Shabbat we often walk to Jerusalem – it is such a beautiful city. I find it hard to relate to someone who has no idea what the Holocaust signified. How could I marry someone if I can't share my feelings with him? What would I say if he left food on his plate - that he has to eat it? Or if he came across my reserves of sugar, flour, soap and so on, how could I explain that?

There is a lot of misunderstanding about what we suffered, and I have become very sensitive about it. Recently our teacher checked our rooms, unannounced of course, to see if we made our beds properly and kept things tidy. Lifting my blanket she said, "Polak! (why can't she call me by my first name?) This bed is not made."

I laughed, because in the camp the Germans regularly checked our beds, and then shouted, "The beds are Scheisse!" (I won't even translate that word!). The poor nurse had a job to do, but I couldn't take her seriously.

Another incident happened in the dermatology outpatient clinic in the city where the relationship between the doctors and nurses was good. One day a very sick child was brought in. He was thin as a rake and terribly sad. And then something unexpected happened: I broke down, sobbing uncontrollably. With difficulty I explained to my upset and worried colleagues, "He looks so much like a boy I nursed in Bergen-Belsen".

They stared at me in shock. "What? You were in Bergen-Belsen?"

Betty, I need more time. Believe me, I am doing my best to lead a normal life, but I have the feeling that the Holocaust will continue to overshadow me for a long time to come.

September 6, 1945

During the High Holidays I always think of our home in Amsterdam. On Rosh HaShana, upon returning from Shul, Father first made Kiddush. We had written a letter, our 'slicha' for Yom Kippur, in which we asked our parents to forgive us for the wrong we had done and promised to be good children in the New Year. After the bracha (blessing) over the bread, Father lifted the covering and acted surprised to find the letters there.

September 10, 1945

On Erev Rosh Hashana many people walk the streets of Jerusalem. Everyone is in a hurry and there is an abundance of flower stalls. Busses are filled to overflowing and everyone greets each other with "Shana Tova!" – "A good year!"

Eliyahu, the number 9 bus driver to Hadassah Hospital pressed my hand so tightly it still hurts.

October 3, 1945

Henrietta Szold died on February 13. She helped create Aliyat haNoar (Youth Aliya) and the hospital on Mount Scopus is named after her. The last years of her life she was nursed in our hospital. Mrs. Szold heard about a student nurse who had been in a concentration camp and asked to see me.

The 84 year-old, very sick woman took my hand and in English asked me to tell her everything about the children in the camp. Never in my life will I forget meeting this woman who had done so much good. After she died, an honour guard stood next to her coffin until the funeral. When my turn came, I kept seeing all those people who died in Bergen-Belsen and who didn't have a grave. At least this very special woman[1] received a royal funeral.

Funeral Henrietta Szold

[1] **Henrietta Szold** (1860 – 1945) was a U.S. Jewish Zionist leader and founder of the Hadassah Women's Organization. When in 1933 conditions for German Jews deteriorated, Szold began to secure visas and transportation for young Jews to move to Palestine. 11,000 young people from Germany and other nations that fell under the Nazi shadow came to Palestine as part of Youth Aliyah. Szold tried to meet every arriving transport of children and took a personal interest in the placement and situation of every child. The childless Szold was recognized by the Jewish world as a true mother in Israel.

I am rather ashamed of what I am going to write now. After the terrorist attack on the King David Hotel, I thought, "What a relief to have a Dutch passport." With this passport I could leave the country any time, but I came to Palestine out of Zionistic ideology. How could I wish to leave? Is it because I have had enough of wars?

Although I saw so much misery and death I still believe that life can be beautiful. I am certain that if I leave this country, for whatever reason, I will not be happy. Don't think that I am going to suddenly get up and leave. It's just that I am shocked at myself for thinking right away of my Dutch passport.

Letter from Jaap (Jack) Polak to Liesje

April 1946

My little sister, I worry about you. From your letters I understand you are meeting all kind of guys. Not that I object, but my dear Liesje, I would feel better if I knew who they were. You're all alone, without parents and neither is your big brother around. Now that our dear Father is gone, I feel responsible for you. Please tell me, what kind of guys are they? Let me give you some advice: Try to find someone from Holland. You'll have the same language and understand each other, something you'll lack if you go out with someone from a different country. And don't choose a kibbutznik – that is not your style. Please continue writing those nice letters and answer me soon. Love, your **brother Jaap (Jack).**

Wedding picture Jaap (Jack) and Ina

Liesje's reply to her brother

My dear Brother,
I received your letter. Thanks for worrying about me!
My dear Jaap (Jack), I know that you are 10 years older than I,
but you forget that your little sister is not so little anymore.
About the Dutch guys: they are BORING, without 'pepper'.
Same language? Don't laugh, but I have almost forgotten my
Dutch and now speak the same language as everyone else:
Hebrew. Please come and visit the land and get to know the
kibbutzniks! They are great guys. Don't worry, dear Brother,
the most important thing is that I marry the man I love[1]. Then,
language is not important, nor if he is a kibbutznik or not.

*With love, your **sister Liesje**.*

[1] Liesje would later marry Hans, who originally came from Germany and lived on a kibbutz .

Travelling by bus is quite an experience!

LETTERS FROM LIESJE TO BETTY

May 17, 1946

Last weekend I visited Netanya on the Mediterranean Sea, a two-hour bus trip. Flowers are blooming everywhere, even on the rocks, and orange plantations begin at the base of the hills and stretch out for kilometers. It was rather nice on the bus. Everyone chatters with everyone else, all the more so with the driver. No signs informing travelers that "It is forbidden to talk to the driver!" People were constantly getting on or off, even where there was no bus stop, but no one was troubled by the delays. Unlike in the Netherlands, everything here is taken in stride.

July 8, 1946

An elderly religious patient asked me if I was a Rabbi's daughter because I brought him water to wash his hands before breakfast. Not wanting to disappoint him I said my grandfather (even though I never knew him) was a famous rabbi. His face brightened and he said, "Du bist a gite Jiddishe Tochter!" (You are a good Yiddishe daughter). A pity Father did not hear that.

August 10, 1946

Today was my last day in the delivery room, and I almost cried that this time is gone. Even though the mothers advised me to never (!) get married, rarely did I work with so much joy. Not only did I learn much, we also laughed a lot during the night shifts. The old midwife I worked with spoke so rudely with everyone that even I blushed. While assisting her, tired and sweating from the effort (as if I was the one giving birth), I suddenly noticed that she had fallen asleep.

August 29, 1946

We suffer from a chamsin, a hot, dry easterly wind. Everyone is tired and sluggish. Outdoors it feels like an oven; Jerusalem is known for its heavy chamsins. The air gets muggy and the sky darkens as if it is about to rain but we won't feel a drop until November.

October 23, 1946

This week we had a Cesarean section. As the nurse rushed away with the small baby, the surgeon called after her, "Come back quickly, there is another one here!" Quite unexpectedly, there were two newly born boys.

January 8, 1947

Last Friday the sky suddenly turned dark as if it was about to rain. But instead it rained hundreds of thousands of locusts. They fell everywhere – in the garden, on the balcony, on the roads and the paths. It was an overwhelming sight!

January 20, 1947

My recent patient was no other than our Prime Minister, David Ben-Gurion! Imagine, I had to give him an injection in his buttocks![1] It was a 'special injection', delivered on a tray, covered with sterile gauze. I entered the room trembling, but he was an affable patient, not at all arrogant. When I asked him if he would like to have something for supper, he answered: "Nothing special, a bit of yoghurt would be fine."

---

[1] Years later I told my young sons that once I had given Ben-Gurion an injection. "*Ima*, what did his 'bum' look like?" they wanted to know. I answered, "I cannot breach patient confidentiality!"

March, 1947

I have been working very hard lately. 17 patients had to get penicillin shots every three hours. Do the math: in eight hours I had to give about 62 penicillin injections. Each time I had to clean, boil and disinfect the needles. I feel like a needle-poking machine.

September, 1947

I have my diploma! This has been a long, difficult journey but I am so happy. As students we wore blue dresses but from now on they will be white uniforms and caps. The day before the ceremony I went to a hairdresser. Your telegram arrived right on time. I received many gifts, and my friends were all happy with the

Liesje (right) proudly wearing her white uniform

Dutch knick-knacks you sent them: the small windmills and the little ceramic klompjes (wooden clogs). What a wonderful feeling to be the first Dutch girl to complete nursing training, and with honors, too! My first concern is to pay back the loans I took out to finance my studies. And then – I will come to visit you.[1]

*Your sister, **Liesje***

---

[1] The intended trip to the Netherlands was postponed until 1962 because of the War of Independence.

JEWISH STATE—*ERETS ISRAEL*

Liesje

November 29, 1947

Certain situations are engraved in my mind, as if they happened only yesterday. One of them was the moment we heard we had our own State – the State of Israel!

Hooked to the radio, I listened to a direct broadcast from the UN building when it was announced who voted for and who was against. And then the last vote: YES! The Jewish people had a home. Everyone went out in the streets to celebrate with singing and dancing. But I was aware of the fact that there was a price tag to this joy. Soon, we would experience the difficult results of the birth of Israel.

I was head nurse of the male surgical ward at Hadassah Mt. Scopus. The first wounded soldiers were brought in, some of them barely 17. These strong and healthy youngsters, who had volunteered to protect their country, were the first victims of the many Arab attacks that followed. Penicillin was the new 'miracle' treatment against infections, but it had to be given every three hours. Day and night I was running to and fro. But it was also 'fun' to have those young boys on the ward, especially when their wounds began to heal.

On May 14, 1948, the State of Israel was born and on the same day the neighbouring Arab nations declared war. All hell broke loose.

The ten minute drive to the hospital on Mt. Scopus passed through the Arab quarter of Sheikh Jarrah. Cars travelling to the hospital were often attacked by the inhabitants of the village, while the British authorities stood idly by. After several such incidents it was decided to only travel to and from the hospital in armoured vehicles. The arrangement made with medical personnel, which was accepted unanimously, was that each member of staff would work in the hospital for three weeks straight, and then spend a week in Jerusalem. We continued this way for several months.

At the end of my week off duty I tidied and cleaned my rented room, and returned to the hospital for my next three week shift. On Monday, 12 April 1948, it was once again time to return to Mt. Scopus. At the pick-up point I was told that the day before mines were discovered along the route. This had prevented the convoy from leaving Jerusalem. As the earlier convoy was to be taken up Mt. Scopus first, we were told to come back the next day.

My friend Siuta, who recently confided to me that she was expecting a baby, was overjoyed at the chance of spending another day at home with her husband. But I had nothing to do in my empty room, with nothing left to eat.

I remained with those who were waiting. One of the drivers, who knew me well (I looked after his wife when she delivered their third child) promised that if there was room in the convoy he would make sure I got in.

At the last moment he pushed me into a corner in the back of his truck. It was a short ride to the top, only a few kilometres. I breathed a sigh of relief when I found myself once again safe and sound on the grounds of the hospital compound.

The Hadassah convoy shortly before the massacre on April 13, 1948

159

From right to left (front row):
Margalith Ben Shalom, Zefona Ashbel and Siuta Appelbaum

Of Blessed Memory ז"ל

My dearest friend **Esther (Siuta) Appelbaum** was born in Romania to a well-educated and wealthy family. Her father was a representative of the Israel National Fund and the chairman of the Zionist Histadrut in their city. During the Second World War, the Soviets captured her father and sent him to Siberia. He never returned. Her mother, aunt (whose husband met a similar fate at the hands of the Soviets), and cousin managed to reach Tchernovitz with Siuta, and from there they travelled to Palestine in 1944 through Turkey, Syria and Lebanon. Siuta's brother was able to flee to Paris. Siuta was a very special person, a good nurse and a charming friend.

Zefona was the daughter of Dov Ashbel, a well-known professor of Meteorology. She was the only one of my fellow students who asked about what happened in Europe. Once she invited me to her home, where I had a very interesting talk with her father and aunt. I will never forget that visit.

Margalit Ben Shalom, the first Yemenite nurse in Hadassah, was born in Jerusalem to a blind father and a mother with poor sight. Her parents had studied in the famous Blind Institute, where her father later taught. They had a shop on Ben Yehuda Street where they sold handmade items made by students in the Institute. Margalit was beautiful, full of the joy of life, and very much loved.

The next day, Tuesday April 13th, at nine in the morning, the personnel expectantly waited to be released from duty by the new shift. But no cars arrived. Hearing the salvo of machine guns and explosions we ran to the balconies. The road was deserted, and columns of smoke rose in the distance. While the convoy was attacked there was nothing we could do but pray that the British would come to their aid. All the vehicles were burned. Most of the people in the convoy perished - professors, doctors, nurses and many others – 78 in all.

Among the dead were three girls from my class – Esther, Zefona and Margalit. (See left page.) To this day I mourn for my friends and all the others murdered in this convoy. May their memory be eternally blessed.

HANS AUERBACH

During the month of August the nursing school was always closed and we students had no choice but to go on leave. The girls eagerly awaited going home to the warmth of their families and to travel around the country. What was I supposed to do for an entire month, alone, without family? Thank heaven for friends. I moved from one kibbutz to another.

Whoever stayed in the kibbutz for more than just a few days was added to the work schedule, so I moved around from one kibbutz to the other. In Kibbutz Galed in the north of Israel I visited my friend, Hadassah, who had arrived in Palestine with me. Deciding it was high time her friend found herself a husband, she had two candidates, and both were truck drivers.

My first date was with Rafael. A nice boy, handsome and not too boring, from Slovakia. After the evening meal we went for a walk.

"Do you know how to drive?"

Before I knew it, I was sitting in the driver's seat and Rafael had his arm around my shoulders. After half an hour I politely told him that I had had enough for the day. Put off by his garlic breath I then and there decided that no husband of mine would be a garlic-eater. Disappointed, he brought me back to my room. Thanking him warmly I quickly shut the door in his face before he could slip into the room after me.

Hadassah didn't give up.

"We have another driver", she said. "He is also handsome, just a bit thin, and he even speaks Dutch...."

Hans didn't find it necessary to teach me how to drive, but taught me other things. He didn't like garlic and we stayed together forever.

As a 14 year-old Hans had been sent from Dresden to Holland with the "*Kindertransport*" after *Kristallnacht.*[1] During the War, the Nazis deported him first to Westerbork and then to Bergen-Belsen. He too survived the "Lost Transport" of Tröbitz. Freed by the Russian Army, Hans returned to Holland. Being a refugee without nationality, he wanted to immigrate to Palestine as soon as possible. After waiting four months in Marseille, France, on March 17, 1946 he embarked on the *Tel Chai.*[2]

---

[1] **Kristallnacht** (Night of Broken Glass or *Pogrom Nacht)* on November 9 and 10, 1938 in Germany and Austria. That night all the synagogues were burnt down. Stores, houses and buildings of Jews ransacked, windows smashed. Many Jews were arrested and immediately transported to notorious concentration camps. It was the beginning of the "Final Solution" and the Holocaust. After these horrible events plans were initiated to save the children. A few months later hundreds of children were sent by train to Holland and much bigger groups travelled to England. Both countries agreed to give them shelter. The British government waived immigration requirements and from December 2nd, 1938 until the beginning of the war in 1939, about 10,000 children from Germany, Austria, Czechoslovakia and Poland were saved. The very last transport left the Netherlands on May 14, 1940.

My new job as a nursing instructor in the large Rambam Hospital in Haifa gave me the opportunity of getting to know my *kibbutznik* (Hans) better.

Every free weekend I spent on the kibbutz, but because Hans shared a room with other bachelors we had to sleep in the beds of absent couples.

The idea of getting married was born from a small tiff. It was rather a slight misunderstanding, for I cannot remember ever quarrelling with Hans. It happened on one of our dates in Haifa.

"I have a day off on Saturday", I told him before he returned to the kibbutz.

"Good," he responded. "But first let me see if there is a room free on that day."

"I just can't keep sleeping in a different bed every time," I burst out. "We must have slept in all the beds on the kibbutz by now!" I didn't say what I really thought – that sleeping in other people's beds wasn't very romantic.

Hans sighed. "I don't know what else to do."

"Maybe we should get married?" I suggested without thinking.

"All right", answered Hans. "But you'll have to come and live on the kibbutz."

"No way! I won't have another couple sleeping in our bed every time we leave the kibbutz!"

---

[2] **Tel Chai**: They reached the shores of Palestine after two difficult weeks at sea. The British authorities, who outlawed Jewish immigration, ordered the boat to land, and brought its passengers to a kibbutz. The *Tel Chai* was the first of about 65 illegal immigrant ships that sought to reach Palestine. Between 1946 and 1948 most of the 70,000 refugees were interned in camps on the Greek part of the island of Cyprus. Others, such as the 4,500 passengers of the *Exodus* were sent back to Europe. They were held in DP camps, which previously had been German concentration camps. The tragic fate of these people, who had escaped the horrors of the Holocaust only to be sent back, drove home to the world the necessity of a Jewish State.

We parted in silence.

Two days later he telephoned me, "There is no room available this Saturday. We'll have to make do with a tent."

"All right then, let it be a tent." At least that was romantic.

On Saturday we talked and decided to get married and start our life together in a new place. It would not be easy, for I still had to pay back my tuition loans. As for Hans, all my beloved had to his name was the iron bed given him by the Jewish Agency, and a few pieces of work clothes. In those days, when a member of the kibbutz wished to leave he was told,

"You're leaving? Go ahead! You will have to make do by yourself. You will get nothing from us."

We began visiting friends to get a feel for other places they lived in. In the end we found a nice *moshav* (cooperative settlement) that was prepared to let us join them, just 30 kilometres north of Haifa.

A rabbi in Tel Aviv who knew my parents was willing to marry us. Fortunately, in 1949, we weren't required to provide birth certificates and other official documents - we didn't have any.

"We have to get rings," I said.

"One ring!" my fiancé hastened to correct me. "We don't have enough money for two."

We took a day off work to make arrangements for our wedding. At the jeweller's I asked to see the most beautiful wedding rings they had.

"Have you lost your mind?" Hans whispered in Dutch. "We only have five liras."

"That's where you're wrong," I said. "We only have two and a half liras. Don't forget, we also have to buy you a pair of new trousers for the wedding. But what difference does it make to you if I just enjoy looking at all these beautiful rings?"

We chose the simplest one of all. It honestly didn't matter to me which one we bought – a ring is a ring.

The wedding took place in Tel Aviv in the house of Aunt Jopie and Uncle Jos (my mother's brother). They also had come to Palestine through the last Templar exchange. Only a few family members and friends were present, but I was overjoyed to see Betty. Travelling all the way from Holland she brought something from 'home' to the occasion. Jaap (Jack) had not been able to come from the USA. After the war, he had divorced Manja and was now happily married to Ina.

I wore the lovely white dress I had bought some years earlier in a moment of weakness. Hans looked very handsome in his new grey trousers and white shirt.

Standing under the *chuppah* I thought about my parents who perished in the Holocaust, my elder sister who also died, and my brother who survived Bergen-Belsen. What a family!

And here I was, the youngest child, getting married. Was this the wedding I had always dreamed of?

I looked at my bridegroom standing next to me under the *chuppah*, his eyes shining. And suddenly I realized that this wasn't just my wedding, it was his too!

What is he thinking? I wondered. He hardly knows anyone here. Is he thinking of his parents who perished in the Holocaust? Of the family he lost? How alone this man is, and I, selfishly dare to feel pity for myself. At least I have a few relatives. He has no one, besides the person he has chosen to be his wife. He looks at me. I look at him. He takes my finger and places the ring on it, saying the ancient words, "Behold, you are consecrated unto me with this ring according to the laws of Moses and Israel." And so we are wed. That was the wedding. No special hairdo for the bride, no fancy hall, no orchestra or four-course meal, no bouquet of flowers and not many presents.

This is how we began our life together. But in that moment under the *chuppah* with Hans, I knew with absolute certainty that we would be there for each other, always, for better or for worse. And we were – for over 63 years[1], in good and bad times, we kept our promise until he died on November 12, 2011 after a short illness.

Liesje and Hans, Tel Aviv, March 17, 1949

After the wedding we lived in *Moshav* Regba, a cooperative settlement. All income went into a joint account and each family received a monthly stipend, depending on the number of family members. Unlike a kibbutz, where the children lived separated from their parents, our children stayed with us. Neither did we have a communal dining room – each family took care of their own meals.

---

[1]At my granddaughter Rotem's wedding in 2013 I said, "Every morning, my husband Hans used to say to me, "Do you know how much I love you?" My wish to you, Rotem and Jonathan, is that you too will continue to say it to each other after 63 years of marriage."

The children had a wonderful life – they grew up free and happy. To us, it felt like we were one big family. Everyone knew each other and when older people began to join the *moshav*, three generations lived together.

In 1956 we left Regba. For the children it had been an ideal place, but Hans could not develop his skills there. Because of the war he did not finish school and never had a chance to learn a profession. As a nurse I could easily find work, so we decided to live from my salary while Hans learned a trade.

From 1959 - 1992, Rishon leZion became our home, until we moved to the assisted living home in Kfar Saba where I still live.

Liesje and Hans and their sons, their wives and children. Maccabim, 2006

SECOND MARRIAGE BETTY

After the war, all the plans Philip and I had made to live as pioneers in Palestine, had lost their meaning. Together we shared the pioneering dream, but without Philip by my side, it became impossible for me. I decided to stay in Holland.

An organization established to assist war survivors who had been active in the resistance offered me a scholarship to go to University. Even though I had lost five years of study during the occupation, I declined the offer. After the war, work was the only cure for the emptiness in my heart.

I had no more than a high school diploma and what I had learned at the Agricultural Institute. Engineer Honig, the director of the specialized fruit farming school, gave me a letter of recommendation to Engineer Van de Plassche, director of the Department of Horticulture in The Hague.

After reading this letter, he explained, "The country is destroyed, people are starving and there is nothing to eat. In the next few years, our agriculture and horticulture will have to provide the solution for our people."

On the spot this man of vision and courage offered me a job. The country was in turmoil without a functioning government and with no way to pay salaries for the time being. Nevertheless, I immediately decided to be part of that organization. We worked over 16 hours a day to rebuild what had been destroyed, to renew contacts in the country and overseas and to organize the supply of food to the famine-stricken country. My colleagues and I worked shoulder to shoulder, even if it meant getting up early in the morning and returning home late at night. The Ministry of Agriculture was housed in a grand building in an affluent Hague neighbourhood which had been badly bombed.

The work was even more interesting than I had imagined. In the ravaged areas I established contacts and disseminated information on the implementation of new developments. The exacting task required vigour, focus

Mushrooms grew in Betty's office

and ambition, but I was full of enthusiasm and energy. Hardly three weeks had gone by when I was informed that my immediate superior was being transferred. He recommended me for his position. During these first years after the war I became the first and only woman to direct a governmental department. Over the years, my field of expertise became larger and more varied.

Israeli delegations frequently visited to learn about new developments. It was a pleasure to accompany them, especially since we could converse in Hebrew. The fascinating work gave meaning to my life. It was exciting and fulfilling, and helped me to repress the memories of the past.

Who would have thought that through my work, and more than ten years after losing Philip, I would find love and the man I wanted to share my life with?

I met Dolf Bausch in 1954 at an international horticultural conference which I attended on behalf of the Ministry of Agriculture. We were supposed to work together, but our work relationship soon blossomed into friendship and love.

Dolf was creative with a wonderful sense of humour; a gifted artist, painter and architect, full of ideas, but also concerned about the welfare of others. It meant a great deal to me that he, too, personally experienced the war and persecution and understood me. At long last we both could lower our guards and allow ourselves to enter into a close, intimate relationship - something that had not been possible until then.

Betty and Dolf marry on January 20, 1961

We married in 1961. Dolf brought two sons from his previous marriage who wanted me to become their new mother. We became a close family.

Dolf had been active in the Resistance, spying on behalf of the Allied Forces, and doing what he could to save his Jewish friends. He was captured and incarcerated in the notorious concentration camp in Amersfoort. Cruel torture resulted in losing a kidney. His life was saved when a German guard let him escape. After liberation he testified on behalf of this German, but his testimony was turned against him. He was wrongfully convicted of collaborating with the enemy and thrown into a camp with suspected Dutch collaborators. While there, his house was ransacked. Only after two dreadful days they discovered the mistake. He could return home.

In many ways our lives had followed parallel paths. When he was troubled by nightmares, I understood why. He could only speak of the war with great difficulty. Alas, our sons know little of what their father achieved during the war. Like many of us, he found it too difficult to talk of the past.

Dolf had to stop working because of his advanced kidney failure. Even the best specialists gave him no more than 6 months, unless he succeeded to have a kidney transplant or dialysis in a hospital. In the 1960's, only young people were selected for dialysis or a transplant. But we did not give up and succeeded in prolonging his life for another 15 years.

At first, Dolf underwent dialysis in a hospital and later through home dialysis, for which we had to attend special courses. Dolf began to study and expand his creativity, resulting in exhibitions at various galleries in the Netherlands and abroad. Many painting found their way to collectors.

We bought a house in Eilat, the beautiful town in the southernmost part of Israel, and enjoyed the wonderful climate to the fullest. It is a pity Dolf never wrote or spoke about his impressive and dangerous work during WWII. He died in December 1982 at the age of 69 and was buried on a mountain overlooking four countries: Israel, Jordan, Egypt and Saudi-Arabia.

He continues to live through his paintings and other art.

Our two sons, two granddaughters and great-grandchildren filled my life with joy. Ruud, the oldest son, passed away in 2012 at the age of 71.

Betty with her sons, Jan Willem (left) and Ruud (center) Kijkduin, 2004

A Different Germany

The almost perfect German I spoke during the war years had been obliterated from my memory. In time I learned to speak it again. At first because of my work connections, and later through dear friendships with Germans who opened my eyes to another outlook, different from what I had experienced.

Being part of an international delegation that was invited by the USA through the Marshall Plan[1] to study "Agricultural Information", new developments of which we had been deprived during the war, my world view changed completely.

The group consisted of representatives from eight European countries. With the war only a few years behind us, the Dutch, French and Norwegians found it difficult to have contact with the Germans or the Austrians. The Yugoslavians, who had been selected from different states, barely talked with each other. The Americans explained the aim of the Marshall Plan: to help the war torn countries to recover, and even more importantly, to form a united Europe. We needed to get to know each other and talk. For the first time I found myself holding intensive conversations, especially with the Germans.

Suddenly realizing my personal preconceptions and prejudices, I reconsidered my attitude towards the enemy.

Don't hate, never ever!

---

[1] **General Marshall** gave his name to a remarkable plan for economic aid and mutual cooperation among 16 free European countries. The organisation for European and Economic Cooperation (E.E.C) has rendered the greatest service of all. But without the massive financial aid provided by the Americans, in spite of hostility on the part of Congress, Europe might well have foundered into ruin and misery.
Excerpt from "The Second World War" by Sir Winston Churchill.

Two out of the group of eight, Klaus Sachsenberg and Klaus von Werder, became my dearest friends. They were of great assistance, not only in composing this book in German, but also in getting it published and promoted. Since then I have raised my voice against discrimination and intolerance, not only in Germany but also in the Netherlands, USA and Israel.

In 1954 the Dutch Government "lent" me to the European Organization of Economic Cooperation (OECE) in Paris to work there in my specialty: Agricultural Information, publications and public relations. Their delegation brought me again in contact with Germans. My work required me to visit Germany often.

Many long years passed before I accepted the invitation of Klaus von Werder to visit Kassel. For the first time I shared my personal war experiences and spoke about my Jewish background, Philip's and my underground activities and even of my attitude towards Germany.

A famous actress reading parts of the script made a great impact. Generalizations can be insidious. I meet many Germans who earnestly try to process the terrible crimes of their country and to reconcile with the past. There, more than anywhere in Europe, the third generation acknowledges the guilt of their country.

Betty with German High school students

Connection to Israel

Even before the State of Israel was established in 1948, I often visited the country. Not only to be with Liesje and her family and my many friends, but also in connection with my work at the Ministry of Agriculture. A lively exchange of publications between Israel and the Netherlands followed (horticulture, flower growing and search results), probably also because of my knowledge of the Hebrew language.

Most of the year I now reside in Israel, not far from Liesje, in Kfar Saba.

Celebrating Jaap (Jack's) 100th birthday on January 14, 2013
Standing: their five grandchildren. On the left: Betty; Liesje on the right.

EPILOGUE

Three "Polak children" miraculously survived the Holocaust during World War II in an astonishing way. Alas, our parents were murdered and Juul, the eldest sister, perished a few days after the liberation in the Eastern part of Germany.

Jaap (Jack), the eldest, Betty, six years younger and Liesje nine years younger, succeeded in starting a new, meaningful life: Jack in the US, Liesje in Israel and Betty in the Netherlands and other countries.

For many years the three of us were unable to speak about our experiences during the Holocaust. Nobody, neither friends or acquaintances, family or children knew anything about what had happened to us during the war.
Much later, dear friends, family members and complete strangers succeeded in convincing us to publish our stories.

First, Jack and Ina published their book, *Steal a pencil for me*, followed by *Broken Silence* by Betty and Liesje, first in Dutch, later in Hebrew and in 2009 in German. From the beginning we strived to realize an even more complete version in English. This took much longer than we had foreseen, mainly due to our advanced age. We are happy and thankful that the enlarged English version finally is available.

Our story had such an impact that invitations to lecture followed, in the US, Germany, the Netherlands and Israel.
The documentary film "Steal a Pencil for me", based on Jaap (Jack) and Ina's book, also contributed to this.

Until today, we share our stories with both large and small audiences. We especially try to inspire youngsters, making them aware of discrimination, intolerance and their consequences.

Survivors, still capable of sharing their stories, symbolize "Living History". As long as health permits, we continue to encourage our youngsters to be optimistic, to embrace life and to be active in helping build a better world.

They are our future.

Life has taken much from us.

Life has given much to us.

Blessed be life.

ACKNOWLEDGEMENTS

In the last 10 years, we, the Polak sisters, published our story in three different languages – Dutch, Hebrew and German.
We realized it should also be translated into English.
However, we hesitated to begin, wondering if we, at our age, should take on the challenge of a new translation.
If it weren't for the energetic and enthusiastic publisher Petra van der Zande, nothing would have come from it. She encouraged and assisted us as much as possible. Many thanks also to her husband, Wim (Bill) for their dedication, patience and determination.

As we wanted the English version to be based on the (expanded) German and the Hebrew edition, we had to find a translator who mastered the three languages.
Rivka Rebecca Nissim was able to do the job while our dear friend Nancy Alroy worked on the finishing touches, as did Dova Aroeti at the Gil Paz retirement home.
We are thankful to all of them.

Also our family and friends, both in England and the USA deserve credit. They eagerly awaited this version and offered their assistance to complete the book. Thank you all for making this story accessible to the rest of the world.

Kfar Saba, May 2014,

Betty Bausch-Polak
Elisheva (Liesje) Auerbach-Polak

PLACE & COUNTRY INDEX

Amersfoort 42,122ff, 126,129,131,170
Amsterdam 6,10,12,15,21ff, 26,31,36ff,
    39ff,42,44,46ff,48,50ff, 52,58,61
    63,78,84,88,91,123ff,134ff,
    144,151
Apeldoorn 35ff,42,123,136ff
Assen 59
Atlit 90,99,115
Auschwitz (ExterminationCamp) 77,79,
    90,96,101,114
Austria 61,162
Balkbrug 120
Bergen-Belsen (Concentration Camp)
    8,51,77ff,79,81ff,90ff,96ff,100
Bilthoven 101ff,111,113
Bosporus 97ff,99
Breedenbroek 97ff,99
Budapest 97
Bulgaria 97
Bussum 4
Celle 79ff,93
Chuliot (Kibbutz) 22
Czechoslovakia 12,162
Dead Sea 148
Den Haag (The Hague) 26,65,68ff,
    136,168
Den Haag, Benoordenhout 68
Deventer 30ff,34ff,44ff, 51,123
Dinxperlo 25ff,28
Drenthe (Province) 59
Dresden 162
Eemnes 22
Eilat 171
Eindhoven 134
England 9,12,28,34ff,102,162,179
France 35,92,101,162
Garderen 21
Germany 10,14,25,47,59ff,78ff,87,90ff,
    94,99,101ff,120,134,143,151ff,
    162,173ff,176
Grebbeberg 27,28

Groenekan 103
Groet 69
Haifa 90,99,163ff
Hannover 79
Hilversum 42
Hoevelaken 127
Hungary/Hungarian 82,96ff
IJssel (River) 30,119
Israel 9,14,21,24,33,35,99,152,158ff,
    161,166,169,171ff,174ff, 176
Istanbul 97
Jerusalem 6ff,139ff,142,150ff,159,160
Kassel 174
Kibbutz Galed 161
Kibbutz Sde Nehemia (Huliot) 22
Kibbutz Yavne 141,147
Kijkduin 172
Lage Vuursche 100
Laren (North Holland) 42ff,52,56,58,69ff
Loenen (Veluwe) 132
Maccabim 167
Marseille 162
Munich 95
Netanya 155
Oegstgeest 118ff,120
Oosterbeek 18
Palestine (British Mandate) 6,9,19,21ff,
    24,31,34,52,63,74ff,77ff,84,90ff,
    92ff,94ff,97,100,115,123
Paris 87,160,174
Poland 37,59,77,162
Prattenberg 129
Regba 166ff
Rhenen 113,129,136
Rosh HaNikra 99
Safed 07
Sloten (Sloterpolder) 23ff,83
Sobibor (Extermination camp)
    77,90,139
Stuttgart 90,99
Tel Aviv 141,164ff
Terwolde 34
The Hague – see Den Haag

Tröbitz 134,162
Twello 30,43
Terwolde 34
USA (United States of America)
122,124,165,173,174,179
Utrecht 103ff,106ff,111,121
Veenendaal 129,130ff
Vienna 92,95ff,102
Vittel 92
Wageningen 126
Westerbork (Transit camp) 8,44,48ff,
54,59ff,63ff,65,69,77ff,79,82ff,
100,139,141,146,162
Zutphen 123

PERSON INDEX
Note: In Holland, a married woman usually takes her husband's family name.
E.g. Betty would sign with: Mrs. Betty de Leeuw-Polak, in that order.

Ader, Bastiaan Jan (Reverend) 130ff
Althoff, A.A.L. (Lex) 47
Althoff, Eduard 47,52
Althoff, Family 55,58
Althoff, Germaine 54,57ff
Amerongen, Jeanne van 124
Amerongen, Truus van 124
Andel, Philip van (Philip de Leeuw)
42ff,108
Andrews Sisters 136
Appelbaum, Siuta 160
Ashbel, Zefona 160
Asscher, Josef (Uncle Jos) 165
Asscher-Morel, Johanna (Aunt Jopie)
165
Asscher-Tal, Betsie (Grandmother) 16
Auerbach, Hans 161ff
Auerbach, Micha 165
Auerbach, Yigal 167
Aus der Fünten, Ferdinand H.
(Hauptsturmführer) 37

Baars, Koos (Architect) 49
Balk, Machiel (Mach) 103,104,112
Bausch, Jan Willem 171
Bausch, Rudolf M.J. (Dolf) 169ff
Bausch, Ruud 171
Ben Shalom, Margalith 160
Ben-Gurion, David (Israel's First Prime
Minister) 156
Bialik, Chaim Nachman (Poet) 144
Boeke, Beatrice 101, 105
Boeke, Kees 101,103,105
Bolle, Godfried (Freddy, brother-in-law)
53,79,81,91,117
Bolle, Max (Evening Cantor) 32,33
Bolle-Polak, Julia (Juul, sister)
10,15,17,53,61,81,91,117,137,1
40,175
Borchardt, Peter (little Peter) 116
Cantor, Shulamit, (Hospital Director)
140,141,146
Chamberlain, A. Neville
(British Prime Minister) 12
Cohen, Eef 30
Cohen, Ernst Herman (Bobby) 50,79
Cohen, Jacques 30
Cohen, Ru 30
Cohen, Ruth 30
Cohen-Gotthelf, Gertrude (Trude) 30,79
Colson (City photographer) 44
Colson-Timmer, Josefine C.L.
(Director Children's Home) 44
Duizend, Bep (cousin) 134
Duizend, Elisheva (daughter of Lida and
Josef) 139
Duizend, Harry (cousin) 135
Duizend, Josef (Joop, cousin) 139
Duizend, Lida 139
Duizend-Hoogstraal, Greet 66,67
Eichmann, K. Adolf (Head security Nazi
Reich) 6,96
Einstein, Albert (German scientist) 124
Gideon (Patient) 87
Gitter, Benno 8,18

Gotthelf, Hede 40
Goudoever, Familie van 68
Goudoever, Henri van (Han) 68
Heertjes, David (Cantor) 31,33
Herzl, Theodor (Founder of political
   Zionism) 19
Hillesum, Etty 37
Hillesum, Misha 36,37
Hitler, Adolf (Führer and Reichs
   chancellor) 10,12,90
Hoff, Pim van der 8
Honig, Dipl. – Ing. H. (School director)
   34,168
Huffener, Joep 101,103,114
Huffener, Lotty 114
Jansen, F. (Gardener) 30
Knoller, Channa 141,142
King Boris (of Bulgaria) 97
Kool, Adrie (Betty) 58,68,71,123
Koole, Ada (Betty) 71,73
Leeuw, Andries A. de (Dries, brother-in-
   law) 34,35,137
Leeuw, Philip de (Flip) 9,21,22,25ff,34ff,
   42,52ff,68,100ff,106,108ff
Leeuw, Suzanna de (Suus, sister-in-law)
   70,118
Marshall Plan (General) 172
Musch, Jo (Betty) 42ff,58
Nabarro, Family (Jacq, Carolina and
   daughter Winnie) 122,126
Neumeier, Hermann 108
Nordheim, Lion 124
Oppenheimer, J. Robert (German
   scientist) 124
Pais, Abraham (Bram) 18,124
Pazner/Posner, Dr. Chaim 77
Pimentel, Beatrice (Bé) 81
Plassche, Dipl.-Ing. A.W. van de 168
Polak, Frederik (Father) 12,15ff,19, 40,
   48,53ff,62,81,144,151,153,155
Polak, Jaap (Jack) (Brother) 8ff,15,17,
   45,47,53,61,80,81,91,135,153,
   154,165, 174,175

Polak-Asscher, Griet (Mother) 15ff,27,
   40,41,54,81,83,93
Polak-Pribludny, Manja (Sister-in-law)
   17,47,80,91,135,136,165
Portielje, Dr. Anton F.J. (Biologist) 17
Queen Wilhelmina van Oranje-Nassau
   137,138
Querido, Dr. Arie and Dr. Tine
   36,37,124
Romein, Prof. Dr. Jan M. and Dr. Annie
   Romein-Verschoor 58,68,72
Roosevelt, Franklin D.
   (President USA) 122
Sachsenberg, Klaus J. 173
Schlottke, Gertrude 78
Soep, Catharina (Ina, sister-in-law)
   8,153,163,174,175
Soldier(s), American & Canadian 135
Soldier(s), German,Nazi 47,49,82,94,
   96,105,121,124,126,127
Soldier(s), British 99
Soldier(s), Dutch 26
Soldier(s), Palestinian 158
Spielberg, Steven A. 7
Steiner, Rudolf J.I. (Austrian
   Philosopher) 68
Szold, Henrietta 140,151,152
Ter Beek, Pieter 11,112
Vecht, Jaap (Jack) (cousin) 46
Werder, von, Klaus Fr. 173
Weide, Julia van der 24
Weide, L.G. van der (Gardener) 23,24,
   67,68
Weizmann, Chaim (First Israeli
   President) 19
Yassky, Chaim, (Director Hadassah
   Hospital) 141
Zecharia (patient) 19

SUBJECT INDEX

Apeldoornsche Bosch, (Psychiatric Institution) 35,35,38,42,136
Ariër Verklaring (Declaration of Aryan Identity) 29,122
Artis (Zoo) 15,17
Balfour, Declaration 19
Boulevard des Misères 60
Chamsin (hot easterly wind, heat wave) 156
Dialysis 171
Diphtheria 65
Evangelische Omroep (Evangelical Broadcasting Company) 8
Exodus (ship) 14,163
Geneva (Conference, City) 28,77
Gestapo (Nazi Secret State Police) 56,57,58,103,123
Shorthand 15
Hachshara (preparation for Palestine) 22,23,30,82,84
Hadassah Hospital 7,140,143,151
HaTikvah (Jewish Anthem) 26,99
Jewish Agency 164
Jewish Hospital (NIZ) 39,48,62,91,134
Jewish National Fund (JNF) 19
Jewish Star (Yellow) 24,29,35,39, 46,83,95,96
Jewish Weekly 26,74
Joodsche Raad (Jewish Council) 74,75
Kidney disease/failure 15,62,170,171
Kristallnacht 162
Kugel (cake) 17
Mastitis 66
Matzos (unleavened bread) 14
Missiles 102,120
Mizrachi (Orthodox-Zionist organization) 18
Moshav (Cooperative Settlement) 164,166
Nazis (Dutch, NSB, collaborators) 42,170
Netherlands War Graves Foundation 133

Orthodox (Jewish) 13,21,84,129
Paleis (Palace) Noordeinde (in Den Haag) 138
Palestine Pioneer (Halutzim) 21,63,168
Palestine Certificate 78,76
Parool, Het (Newspaper) 47,106
Passover/Pesach 14,124
Philips- Factory 134ff
Psalms, David 106
Rambam Hospital 163
Revier (District, hospital barracks in Bergen-Belsen) 82,85
Red Army 134
Red Cross 77,95ff,106
Royal Air Force (RAF) 35,137
Royal Concert Hall (Amsterdam) 22,88
Royal Police Corps (Koninklijke Marechaussee) 131
Shabbat (Sabbath,Saturday) 13,16,17, 31, 53,62,139,144,150,163,164
Sabra(s) 143,144
Seder meal 14,124
Specialized School of Fruit Growing 34
Sukkot (Feast of Tabernacles) 13
Tel Chai (ship) 162, 163
Templar(s) 90,99,165
University, Amsterdam 21,168
University, Hebrew (Jerusalem) 140
V1 and V2 Rockets (German) 120
Werkplaats, De (School) 101
Yad Vashem 114
Yekkes (Yekim) 143
Yemenite 147,160
Zichron Ya'akov (Youth Organisation) 31
Yom Kippur (Day of Atonement) 31,32,151
Ziele, de (Agricultural Farm) 30,34

For additional stories related to this book,
please go to:

http://bettyandelisheva.blogspot.co.il